पुरामंथन
PURĀMANTHANA

पुरामंथन

PURĀMANTHANA

(CURRENT ADVANCES IN INDIAN ARCHAEOLOGY)

Number : 4 **2006**

Editors

A.K. SHARMA

B.R. MANI

G.S. KHWAJA

Advisor

JAGAT PATI JOSHI

BKP

BHARATIYA KALA PRAKASHAN

DELHI (INDIA)

First Edition : 2007

Published by **C.P. Gautam**
BHARATIYA KALA PRAKASHAN
3421-A, IInd Floor, Narang Colony, Tri Nagar,
Delhi-110035. Phone : 27393083, 32967505
E-mail: bkp3421@yahoo-co.in

ISBN : 978-81-8090-165-2

Laser Type Setting by
A-One Graphics,
Pitampura, Delhi-110088

Printed at :
BDH Printer at Salasar Imaging System, Delhi-35

Editorial

Puramanthana No.4 is before you. Please don't mind the shortcomings. We are bringing out your magazine for you, without any financial help from anybody.

Presently archaeology in India is in a state of turmoil. Not much of fieldwork is being done. Epigraphy is in a bad shape. The number of students going for archaeology in universities is dwindling. Instead of paying more attention to conservation, budget is being spent on secondary aspects. Bureaucracy is trying to dictate technocrats. We are ourselves to blame for this sorry state of affairs. It is upto young scholars to rise to the occassion and salvage archaeology. As Mother Terresa said "Do not wait for leaders, do it alone person to person." Archaeology is five percent inspiration, 25 percent commonsense, seventy percent perspiration. Hard work and fieldwork is the only way. Create habit of writing your observations, your findings and thoughts and send it to us. We are for you.

With your co-operation we will be able to contribute substantially by the time we celebrate 150 years of A.S.I. in 2011.

—A.K. Sharma

Contents

List of Figures

List of Plates

1

Discovery of a New Copper Hoard Site at Village Atwa in District Moradabad (Uttar Pradesh)

*—Dr. Krishna Kumar**

I. Introduction :

The Ochre Coloured Pottery (hereafter, OCP) represents one of the earliest protohistoric cultures that flourished in the Upper Gaṅgā valley in the time-bracket of c. 2100-900 B.C[1]. with a margin on earlier side. The Gangetic Copper Hoards are closely associated with this culture. Of the various copper hoard objects, the anthropomorphic figurines are perhaps the most eniquatic ones. A new hoard exclusively comprising of six anthropomorphs has recently come to light from village Atwa in district Moradabad (Uttar Pradesh). Since these figurines represent a new type, I have briefly described and illustrated them and discussed their significance in this paper.

II. Discovery :

The hoard was incidentally found by Deva Raj Singh while digging a pit in the agricultural field of Rishi Pal Singh at village Atwa in P.S. Kurha Fatehpur, Tahsil Chandausi (28° 27' N-78° 47' E), District Moradabad (U.P.) on 16th July 2004. The hoard was confiscated by the local police and as per orders of the District Magistrate it was transferred to the State Museum, Lucknow, where the hoard is being chemically cleaned in the laboratory. According to Mahavir Singh Chauhan, chemist, a hard and thick deposition of calcareous matter was the main encrustation on the object. Underneath the calcareous deposition a smooth layer of green patina was noticed. The chemical test of the corrosion product yielded carbonate and trace of chloride ion.

* Former Dy. Superintending Archaeologist, Archaeological Survey of India, 184, Qaziyana, Kotwali Road, Fatehpur-212601 (U.P.)

III. Hoard :

The Atwa hoard consists of the following six figurines :

(i) This is the lightest object in the hoard. It is distinguished by extraordinarily elongated outstretched pointed legs, horizontally extended sharp arms with slightly curved hands and a broad high semicircular head outlined by a thick regular ridge. One leg is little longer than the other. The surface does not show chased patterning as noticed on other examples. One arm was intentionally broken by the discoverers evidently to test the metal. It bears green patina. Typologically, it closely resembles with the copper anthropomorph from Fatehgarh, now preserved in the Indian Museum, Calcutta[2]. Size : App. 56.9 ×34.00 ×0.5 cm. Weight: App. 1.780 kg. (Fig.1-I).

(ii) This is the smallest specimen in the hoard. It has extraordinarily elongated outstretched pointed legs, horizontally extended sharp arms with slightly curved hands and a roughly semi-circular large head outlined by a thick regular ridge. The surface does not bear chased patterning as noticed on other specimens. One leg is comparatively short and thin than the other. The shorter leg was slightly damaged before the deposition of the hoard in distant past. A big chunk of a sharp arm including hand has been intentionally broken by the discoverers to test the metal. It bears green patina. Size: App. 52.00 ×35.4 ×0.5 cm. Weight: App 1.950 kg. (Fig l. II).

(iii) This is the largest example in the hoard. It is characterized by exceptionally elongated outstretched pointed legs, horizontally extended sharp arms with slightly curved hands and a roughly broad high head outlined by a thick regular ridge. The surface displays chased patterning. It is a well-preserved specimen covered with green patina. Size: App. 62.2 ×40.9 ×0.4 cm. Weight : App. 2,300 kg. (Fig. l. III).

(iv) This is the heaviest piece in the hoard. It has extraordinarily elongated outstretched pointed legs, horizontally extended sharp arms with slightly curved hands and a broad high head outlined by a thick regular ridge. The surface shows chased patterning. It is a well-preserved object covered with green patina. Size: App.58.5 ×43.5 ×0.8 cm. Weight : App. 3.180 kg. (Fig. l. IV).

(v) It is characterized by exceptionally elongated outstretched pointed legs, horizontally extended sharp arms with slightly curved hands and a broad high head outlined by a thick regular ridge. The surface shows chased

I

II

III

IV

Fig. 1 Atwa : Anthrepomorphic figures

V

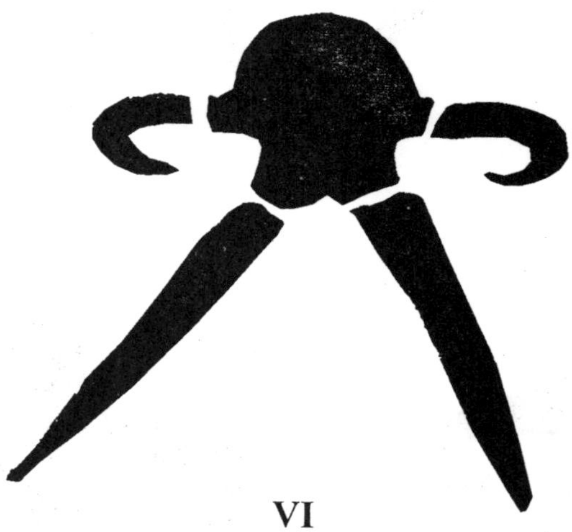

VI

Fig. 2-Atwa : Anthrepomorphic figures

patterning. It is a well-preserved object covered with green patina. Size: App. 56.1 ×41.00 ×0.7cm. Weight : App. 2.570 kg. (Pl. V).

(vi) This piece has been intentionally broken by the discoverers just to test the metal. Some portions of the broken arms are missing. It is characterized by exceptionally elongated outstretched pointed legs, horizontally extended sharp arms with slightly curved hand and a broad high head outlined by a thick regular ridge. The surface shows chased patterning. It is a well-preserved object covered with green patina. Size: App. 58.00 ×18.9 ×0.5 cm. Weight : App. 2.80 kg. (Fig. 1. VI).

From the foregoing description, it is evident that all the figurines characterised by exceptionally elongated outstretched pointed legs represent one single type. However, one specimen, i.e. number (i) Fig. 1, slightly differs from rest of the figurines in respect that it has a large semi-circular head, whereas the remaining figures show a roughly broad high head.

IV. Discussion :

The importance of the present hoard lies in the fact that it hails from village Atwa, which is situated not far from village Madarpur, where a large hoard comprising of 31 anthropomorphic figurines was incidentally discovered on 7th January 2000.[3] Typologically, both the hoards are quite different. It appears that during the protohistoric times there existed two workshops, one at Madarpur and the other at Atwa. The copper smiths of both the workshops exclusively manufactured anthropomorphic figurines of different varieties and supplied them for sale to different places. This observation receives some support from the fact that as noticed above a copper anthropomorph closely resembling the figurine number (i) Fig. 1, of the Atwa hoard was found at Fatehgarh in 1883.[4] The Fatehgarh example, however, differs from the Atwa specimen in respect that the former bears chased patterning on both the sides. This feature is however not noticed on the Atwa figurine referred to above. Even today brass vessels manufactured at Moradabad are exported for sale to distant places. Thus the antiquity of the metal craft of Moradabad goes back to the protohistoric times. D.V. Sharma, the excavator of Madarpur, observed the contemporaneity of the copper hoard with the OCP without any ambiguity.[5]

Although no information is available regarding the occurrence of the OCP at Atwa, there is a strong probabilty that if the find-spot is thoroughly examined we may get OCP sherds there also.

The difference in shape, size and weight of all the six objects suggests that they were separately made keeping in view the requirements of the customers. As enumerated elsewhere, seven types of the copper anthropomorphs are known to the scholarly world.[6] However, the newly discovered Atwa hoard has rendered the typological classification of these figurines eightfold. These figurines most probably represent the images of lord Indra, the first and foremost god of the late Ṛgvedic Aryans.[7] As noticed above in four examples the surface shows chased patterning. This feature has also been noticed on the copper anthropomorphs discovered elsewhere[8]. The thin lines chased on the surface most probably symbolise the rays of divine power (*tejas*) emanating from the body of lord Indra[9]. The horizontally stretched arms of these figurines were intentionally sharpened, because they were plausibly employed in magical rites probably meant for *abhichāra* purpose i.e. inflicting harm or to kill the enemies.[10] In these rituals the clay effigies of enemies were slain with the aid of sharp arms of the copper anthropomorphs.[11] Their toes were purposely made pointed to conveniently fix them on altars before the commencement of worship.[12]

ACKNOWLEDGEMENT

The author's grateful thanks are due to Shri Jitendra Kumar, Director, State Museum, Lucknow for extending all possible help and cooperation in the course of present study. The copyright of the photographs (Fig. 1) published here rests with the State Museum, Lucknow.

REFERENCES

1. Krishna Kumar, *Studies in the Ochre Coloured Pottery Culture,* Unpublished D. Phil. Thesis, University of Allahabad, 2001, p. 263.
2. J. Anderson, *Catalogue and Handbook of the Archaeological Collections in the Indian Museum (Calcutta)*, 1883, p. 408.
3. D.V. Sharma, et al, 'A Report on Excavation at Madarpur, A Copper Hoard Site', *Puratattva,* 32. 2001-2002, p. 34.
4. V.A. Smith, 'The Copper Age and Protohistoric Bronze Implements of India', *Indian Antiquary,* 34, 1905, pp. 232, 238, Pl. 5.
5. D.V. Sharma, et al, 2001-2002, *op.cit.,* p. 37.
6. Krishna Kumar. 'The Typology and Identification of Protohistoric Copper/Bronze Anthropomorphs: An Assessment in the Light of New Evidence', *Pragdhara,* 12, 2001-2002, pp. 127-32.
7. Krishna Kumar. 'The Beginnings of the Brahmānical lconography in the Gaṅgā Valley', *Journal of the Indian Society of Oriental Art,* New Series, XXII & XXIII, 1993-1995, p. 56.

8. Paul Yule, *Metal Work of the Bronze Age in India,* Munchen, 1985.
9. Krishna Kumar, 1993-1995, *op.cit.,* pp. 36&37.
10. J.N. Banerjea, *The Development of Hindu Iconography,* New Delhi, 1974, p. 59
11. Krishna Kumar 1993-1995, *op.cit.,* pp. 44-45.
12. *Ibid.,* p. 37.

2

Indian Migrants in West Asia and Central and South Africa : A Clue

—*Dr. Arun Kumar**

The Bṛhaspati *sūkta* of *Ṛgveda* says in its very first *mantra* that (after the creation was complete) "he first installed the speech-language bearing the names of all the created objects into the depth of the *ṛṣis*. His noble act of speech-language installation was really sinless"[1] When I first studied this, I was ever wondering why such noble act as imparting instructions in the intricacies of language inspired the seer of this *sūkta* to be so apologetic as to take special care to call it "sinless". However, this puzzle was soon solved after I read the following statement in the Śatapatha Brāhmaṇa. It quotes a *śloka* "those good gods, digging deep into the sea (of the brain) with a sharp instrument installed the knowledge therein"[2]

These two statements, in conjunction with another, occurring, again, in the same *brāhmaṇa,* gave me a clue to understand the whole problem. It is said that the gods, whosoever they may have been, while roaming this earth of ours found the *puruṣapaśu* closest to them in physical appearance and size.[3] And becoming curious they caught him.[4] He was, however, found to be only a speech-and-thought less animal, the only difference being its lack of horns. As it was very much alike them in physical appearance, they thought it prudent to operate upon its brain and install the speech-language mechanism. As this operation involved the cutting to open the brain box, in which blood must have flowed, the seer of the above referred to *mantra* had to take special care to declare it 'sinless'; it was in the intrest of the one cut open.

Again, some *mantras* in other *saṁhitās* seem to suggest that once this speech-thoughtless *puruṣa-paśu* was transformed into a thoughtful *manuṣya*-man, he was set

* Former Dy. Superintending Archaeologist, ASI.

to procure the much needed sustenance for the *devas,* his masters, so that they may pursue their other pursuits full time. Thus it is said :

> This victim, O Lord of Cattle, for the today,
> I bind, O Agni, in the *midst of righteous action:*
> Approve it, and let us offer with a good offering;
> May this offering be welcome to the gods.[5]
> What cattle, the Lord of Cattle ruleth,
> Both the four-footed and the two-footed,
> May he, bought off, go to his offering share
> May abundance of wealth fall to the offerer.[6]
> The cattle of the forest, of all forms
> Of various forms, many of one form.
> Let the god Vāyu, first release them,
> Lord of offspring, in harmony with the offspring[7]
> Let it go alive to the place of the gods;
> Fulfilled may the desires of the offerer be.[8]
> With the *ghee* do thou strengthen the bodies,
> May the gods eat the offering made with the cry of *svāhā* ![9]

In the *Atharvaveda,*[10] too, a somewhat similar *mantra* repeats the sentiments expressed in the second of the above quotes. It is truly said that man has many desires that know, no limit—*pulukamo hi mariyaḥ*[11].

All these evidences, howsoever scanty they may seem, are clearly suggestive of the fact that once the *puruṣa paśu* was transformed into a thinking animal, he was entrusted with the task of gathering the animals for his overlords. He, however, was not yet intelligent enough to select the needed ones. He captures everything and let the lord retain the desired ones and release the others.

This suggestion of ours, ever since it was published,[12] has been considered to be too farfetched to be considered even a plausibility. It was, therefore, summarily rubbished. But the information enshrined in the traditions of other old civilizations seems to confirm our imaginative approach. Thus, in the Sumerian myth Enki "creates human being who was feeble in mind and body".[13] Its extended version contained in the Babylonian Epic of Creation mentions that Kingu is slain and from his blood mankind is created "for the service of the gods, to till the ground and free the gods from having to work for their living". Both the sets of information are almost the same, but for the introduction of tillage in the latter, which speaks not only of its posteriority in time but of an advanced stage of civilization.[14]

Once the man-*manuṣya* i.e., *homo sapienṣ* was created he became prolific producer and soon populated the world. The story of mankind, as seen from the perspective of Indian Historical Tradition has already been told. Moving down the memory lane, we come to the story of *Dāśarajña*, the battle of ten kings that happened almost at the junction of *Tretā* and *Dvāpara*. During the course of this fiercely fought battle, when each contender was loudly hailing the same gods for succour, the rise and ebb of the river waters that sometimes engulfed the chariot wheels and at others they became easily passable,[15] indicated perhaps the sporadic upheavals in the mountains, which were their source. From the later history as deduced and reconstructed by us, it appears that within a couple of generations after the battle, the whole land falling between Sindhu and Gaṅgā, comprising the Saraswatī and its five tributaries[16] and the beleaguered people had to flee for safety to either east or west. To the east, there was a vast landscape to absorb the refugees, but in the west, especially north-west, in broken and inhospitable valleys of Afghanistan only so much of the refugees could be absorbed and the rest had, of necessity, to move further north into the Central Asian plains. Making this area their main refuge, they slowly moved north and west and thereby influenced the cultures of those regions and left a lasting imprint on the language[17] and literature.[18] In the absense of archaeological proof the traces of their impact on these two constitute all the evidence, which, however, gives us fairly clear idea of the incoming of the Indian diaspora.

Here, however, we are not concerned with the detailed analysis of this evidence, which has satisfactorily been done by Dr. Ram Vilasa Sharma in the two books referred to above. I would rather concentrate here only on the story of the Flood, as contained in Indian-Vedic-and partially known where it is described how Enki declares his intention to save the mankind from the destruction which the gods have decided to bring upon them. Thereafter,

> "After, for seven days (and) seven nights
> The Flood had swept over the land"

and the huge boat that Ziusudra, 'the preserver of the name of vegetation (and) of the seed of mankind' had launched at the behest of Enki, found shelter

> "In the land of crossing, the land of Dilmun, the place. Where the sun rises, they caused to dwell".

This myth has been considerably enlarged in its Babylonian-Akkadian version. Here Ea reveals to Utnapishitim, that the gods design to destroy all the seeds of life by flood, and he was to save them by bringing "the seed of all living things" in a ship. The latter, however, according to the dimensions given, must have, instead of a boat or ship, been a building in the from of a perfect cube. It is, therefore, quite plausible that this was only a staged tower called '*Ziqqurat*', which were a regular feature of the temple building, and were originally designed as a place of refuge from the frequent floods in the Delta.[21] Be whatever it may, the ship grounds on Mt. Nisir and the inhabitable land is found through a raven-*diśākāka* and they settle far away at the mouth of the river.[22]

Before we begin our analysis of the above evidence, let us mention that at the far western extremes of Asia from Abisinia in Africa to Constantinople in Asia Minor the creation is placed at 55 years before Christ. Thus Abisinians start it at 5493, Alexandrians at 5502, in Antioch at 5492 and in Constantinople at 5508. The last was suppressed by Peter the Great of Russia, but it has continued secondly, as the original Dilmun of the Sumerian mythology was identified by Kramer with the lower reaches of the Sindhu-Sarasvatī valleys,[31] the whole episode seems to have been based on the memory of the story of Manu.[32] Thirdly, the suggestion that the ship of Utnapishtim was nothing but the '*ziqqurat*' designed as a place of refuge from the frequent floods in the delta of Euphrates and Tigris, is not that doubtful as Hook makes us to believe. The tradition of building such cubical platforms appears to have started in Mehrgarh, in levels dated to pre 5000 years B.C. and continues as late as the latest mature Harappan sites in the Sarasvatī[33] valley. Here it would not be out of place to mention that in the liturgies Tammuz and Ishtare are frequently represented under the figure of a male and female 'fir tree' As the 'fir' does not occur in Iraq, it must have been the Sumerians' way to reminisce about their original homeland. And the only place that both abounds in the tree and must have also been affected by the Sarasvatī floods of 'unusual severity' is the Sindhu-Sarasvatī high land.

Next in antiquity is the Egyptian civilization. While the flooding of the Nile could at times be excessive, there was nothing in Egyptian or for that matter among the other cultures of the west Asiatic region, which corresponded to the destructive flood. It is, therefore, that the memory of the devastations caused by the flood lost its grip on the public mind and soon the tradition was lost. In the creation myth of Egypt, however, Path (*prajāpati* or *pitaḥ*?)[34] brings gods into existence, and order out of chaos. His creative activity is closed with the words: "and so Path rested (or was satisfied) after he had made everything".[35] It is perhaps a fair echo of the Brahmanic statements.[36]

Next in antiquity were the Hitittes, the non-semitic migrants who settled in Asia Minor about the beginning of the third millennium B.C. and built up an empire that lasted until c. 1225 B.C.[37] That they came from India is almost certain only because they worshipped such Vedic deities as Indra, Varuṇa and the twins Nasatyau, retained Kikkuli, the Mitanni, to write a treatise, full of Sanskrit terms, on horse training and also to train their horses, introduced, in a land that had so far used only ass-driven chariots mounted on solid wheels, a horse-driven chariot with a *ṣadacakra*-sixspoked wheel.[38] Prof Gurney, believing in the fallibity of the pronouncement of Max Müller on the date of Ṛg Veda, however, laments the failure of European scholarship to arrive at the solution to the vexed problem of the date and the route followed by these earliest penetrations of the Indo-Europeans (Indians) into Asia Minor.[39] Though more than 10 thousand tablets have been discovered at Bogazkoy alone, they are in such a fragmentary state that no more than three legends could be reconstructed with a semblance of completion and, therefore,we do not find any story of creation or flood.

Of these three legnds, while that of Ullikammis, otherwise known as 'slaying of the Dragon' tells of goddess Inaras who sleeps with a mortal Hupasiyas in order to lure him to help the gods kill the dragon. She later builds a house for Hupasiyas on the rock in the district of Tarukka. Here Hupasiyas was installed with the instruction not to open the window and she went out on a sojourn. After waiting for 20 days Hupasiyas could contain no more and opening the window saw his wife and children. On her return the goddess, finding him having not kept the faith, punished him by desertion or destruction.[40]

The story is said to exemplify the love of immortal for the mortal and the latter's desire to revert to his earthly family. The resemblance, however, between it and that of Pururavās and Urvaśī as told in the Veda and again by Kālidāsa in *Vikramorvaśīyam* is evident. Both the heroes helped the gods, gained the possession of a divine damsel who imposes certain conditions for a lasting relationship and when the condition is breached, she punishes them by desertion or destruction. If, however, Hupasiyas was really killed and not only destroyed by desertion, it may only be a reflection of the impoverished conditions of the erstwhile peaceful city dwellers. In the story as told in the Veda, Pururavās offers to kill himself by offering his body to feed the wolves.[41] The Devine damsel, Urvaśī, however persuades him not to take such a drastic measure, for 'there can be no lasting friendship with women, they have the hearts of hyenas.[42] It, therefore, seems certain that the legend was carried from India abroad and got transformed during the course of long sojourn to its present level.

The other legend of the missing God or the story of Telepinus describes the paralysis of all life on earth caused by the disappearance of the god of fertility and agriculture. The description of the blight is as follows:

> "Dust (?) clouds beset, the window, smoke (?) besets the house, the embers on the hearth were choked (?), The gods stifled (in the temple), the sheep stifled in the fold, the oxen stifled in the stall, the ewe spurned her lamb, the cow spurned her calf......Barley and emmer wheat throve no more, oxen, sheep and humans ceased to conceive, and those who were pregnant could not bear".
>
> "Trees withered and the meadows and springs dried up. So there was a famine, and both gods and man began to starve".

"We must act at once, (or else) we shall die of starvation"[43] was the consensus among the gods. Search for the god of fertility and agriculture. Telepinus, who 'harrows, ploughs, irrigates the field and makes the crops grow' begins with the help of Hasammelis, the god who protects the travellers, and the missing god is eventually found in a far away country.

The above quoted description of the blight reads much the same as that from the *Mahābhārata* that reports the conditions in the draught affected Sarasvatī valley.[44] As the Hitittes are certain to have moved out of India, both the earlier destruction by flood and the later devastation by draught seem to have coalesced together and the recent one, fresh in the memory got the upper hand. The finding of the god of fertility and agritulture in a far away land with the help of the god of travellers suggests only the migration to a far away land fertile enough to settle in.

In another version, contained in the Yuzgat tablet, of the story, the blight is ascribed to hahhimas, torpor, who had "paralysed the whole earth, --- dried-up the waters, --- is mighty".[45] Though no certainty can be claimed, the word '*hahhimas*' sounds much like '*hima*' short of '*himavanta*' and may, therefore, refer to the inactivity of the rivers, which had dried up due to the upheavals in the Himālayas. Otherwise the 'inactivity' will be due to the draught, when the people had nothing to do.

As remarked by discerning scholars, this search for the missing god of fertility and agriculture is closely paralled in the literature associated with the saga of Adonis (Greek) Attis, Osiris (Egypt) and Tammuz (Akkad). Now, they are the typical of the myths of the annual spring festivals.[46] But surprisingly enough none of these texts are explicitly connected with the seasonal festivals. Hence, there is every likelihood that, like the Jewish feast of 'Passover' which celebrates their passage from Egypt to Israel, these festivals continued to commemorate the original search for fertility, i.e. the fertile lands after their own was rendered inhabitable by flood or devastated by the draught.

Now turning to the specifically Semitic mythology, we find that the Hebrews have lost much that concerned with the creation *ex nihilo* and remained content with only the problem of bringing order out of the existing chaos. But the source or sources of the Palestinian myths, which the Yahwist authors used were the Egyptian and the Sumerian myths, with whom they were in contact during their captivity. Thus the planting by Yahweh of 'garden in Eden, to the East'[47] seems to recall the memory of the Mesopotamian Dilmun. It is said that the Eden of this myth belongs rather to the "land east of the sun and west of the moon" than to any concrete geographical locality. The Akkadian word *edinu* means 'plain' or 'steppe'.[48] In one place[48] the garden is placed in the mountain of the gods, a concept which occurs in the Ugaritic myth. The idea of the dweller in the garden as the embodiment of wisdom is referred to in Job,[50] where the first man is described as the possessor of wisdom and as having heard the secret counsel of God.

Many scholars hold the view that the semi-mythical geography of Paradise does not belong to the Yahwist narrative but is an editorial gloss confusing very ancient ideas about the location of Paradise. Here, too, while the garden's emplacement in the mountain of the gods reminds at once the *Kailāśa-Mānasarovara* area in the Himālayas, its residents' embodiment of wisdom surely points to the Vedics being the seers who were supposed to have been enlightened by the god or gods themselves.[51] So far as the 'plain' or 'steppe' is concerned, it may refer to the sandy plains of the lower Sarasvatī valley.

Here we must necessarily revert to the Sindhu-Sarasvatī valley and recall the happenings there. After the flood mentioned above had receded, the foundations of the Kuru-dynasty were laid. Towards the end of the *Dvāpara* the fratricidal war was fought between the two branches of the same family. The ensuing millennia witnessed both the efflorescence and decline and then demise of this Kuru Empire that was none other than the Harappan culture of the Sindhu Sarasvatī valley.[52] Its downfall seems to have started with the shifting of the rivers and the final drying up of the water resources hastened its demise and started the exodus. The main cause of this drying up was the seismic activities in their source areas, the Himālayas,[53] which resulted in a long lasting drought in the Sarasvatī valley. It has been opined that this draught was a pan-Asiatic, if not a global, phenomenon that extended from the western most limits of Asia to the Central Asia and hastened the demise of almost all other ancient civilizations of the region.[54] Recently, however, it has been demonstrated that a volcano had erupted somewhere in Asia Minor or beyond in the Mediterranean and its spreading acidic ash had formed a thin film over most of the land from Asia Minor to Central Asia and possibly also the Sarasvatī valley, rendering it infertile and unproductive.[55]

This surmise of volcanic eruption seems to find confirmation from the Biblical accounts of the destruction of the wicked cities of Sodom and Gomorrah, effected by an 'overthrow', a word which in Hebrew usually described the effects of an earthquake and the subsequent rain of fire and sulphur from the heavens.[56]

This episode of long draught is remembered in the Ugaritic legends as the absence of Baal for seven years. These legends, though written down only in the 14th century B.C., contain myths of much earlier origin.[57] However, these remnants of an urban society remembered their glorious past long after they were reduced to the nomadic or village life style. Though archaeological proof for this exodus is lacking, on the basis of comparative linguistics Dr. Sharma has shown that while the word for 'village' in the various regional languages of Europe is always different, the word for city all over Europe is only a derivatie from Sanskrit '*pura*'. He, therefore, concludes that the people introducing the word and concept of the *'pura'* i.e., city to the savages of Europe must have once experienced it in their native land and says that in those days it was only the Sarasvatī valley which had witnessed both the efflorescence of the urban life as well as the Sanskrit language containing the word *'pura'* in its vocabulary.[58]

These *'pura'* refugees, moving along with their herds of cattle, in search of fresh pastures must have encroached upon the fertile land and the original feud between the nomads during the earlier exodus, when the host lands were not the least effected, was renewed with much severity. This led to the story of Cain, the farmer and Abel, the shepherd. Among the Palestinians the legend is artifically linked up with the myth of Paradise. The legend of Cain and Abel has various strands and all were originally distinct, none having any connection with the myth to which they are attached now to weave a homogeneous tapestry of the Biblical myth, in which Abel, the shepherd is eventually killed.[58]

The second part of the story concerns itself with probably the fragments of the earlier traditions of the Kenite clan. The long standing connection of the Kenites with the Hebrews goes back to the saga of Moses, who is represented as having married into the Kenite clan. Be what it may, they were always nomads or half-nomadic tent dwellers.[60] Their ancestors, however, depicted in this part of the myth as "a city-builders, were settled inhabitants of a land which cannot be identified geographically".[61] This difficulty in identifying the land is almost certainly created by the scholar's penchant for the chronology proposed by Max Mueller and, therefore, not heeding to the saner advise of O.R. Gurney, who had proposed to bring the Hittites from India. From what we have said above it must now have become abundantly clear that the city dwelling ancestors of the Kenites must have come from the land of the Harappan cities in the Sarasvatī valley and had perforce to adopt to pastoral way of life under the changed circumstances. They, however, continued to remember their once glorious past.

Hebrews are supposed to be of Semitic origin. It is perhaps because of their language and culture, but much of their culture must have been imbibed during their captivity in Egypt and then in Mesopotamia-Akkad-Assur. However, as Alfred Guillaume has observed:

> "in and around Egypt and middle Euphrates (c. 2000 B.C.) and in Palestine and Syria (c. 1400 B.C.) we find that hordes of tribesmen notorious for brigandage were a constant menace to the civilized settlements. These people or peoples were known as *Habiru* (or *Apiru*) and are almost certainly to be identified with the Arabs. If that be so, then the Hebrews of the Old Testament were Arabs, part of the ancient inhabitants of the Arabian peninsula. No convincing explanation of

> the name Arab has ever been proposed; but if we adopt this identification the meaning of *Arab* a metathetical form of *Abir* is 'nomad'. This identification is supported by the meaning which the plural a "*rab*=nomad often has in the Quran and in the inscriptions found in South Arabia which mention Bedouin".[62]

Though the Arabists could find no convening explantation for the name Arab, its various pronouncements as given by Guillaume himself as well as that of Ophir, occurring in the Bible, seem to link them to the Ābhiras in India. Here it would not be out of place to mention that while Ābhira gave rise to such words as Apir, Abira and Arab as well as Habiru, the latter was transformed in India to "*Habura*" just in the same manner as Uzbeka to '*ujabak*' in Hindi. In ancient Indian literature they are said to have once lived on Indus. In the Viṣṇu *purāṇa* an Ābhira dynasty is reported to have closely followed the Āndhrabhṛtyas. In Manu they are declared to be the progeny of a Brāhmaṇa husband and an Ambaṣṭha wife. But there was no social stigma attached to them. The author of Periplus (c. 100 A.D.) found them already settled. Ābhira Rudrabhūti (c. 181 A.D.) was the general of the western Kṣatrapas. Another Ābhira Īśvarasena ruled a principality near Nasik (c. 300 A.D.). By the time of Samudragupta (c. 350 A.D.) they occupied the adjacent areas in Rajasthan and Malwa. Neither their names nor their language, which Bharata in his Nāṭyaśastra calls 'Ābhirokti', leaves any doubt about their being the sons of the soil.[63] If this equation is accepted then the Ābhiras from the Sindhu valley must have moved east and west during the long drawn daught that effected the Sarasvatī Valley. Referring back to the Brahmānic evidence of the drying up of the river, [64] Manu says that during the draught the Ābhiras had moved to the area near Vinasana where it was lost in the sea of sand.

The Jews start their year from 3760 B.C. The day the Jewish state was announced on 11th May 1948, it was the 5th Sabbath of their *lyar* 5708, according to which that year must have begun on 10th April. Therefore it is likely that they followed the Indian custom of starting the year with the first day of the bright half of the month of *caitra* which falls thereabouts. Though the memory of the blight and the feud between Cain and Abel seems to link their emigration to the Sarasvatī draught, it is not unlikely, that they had to migrate even earlier due to some unknown political pressure. It is not improbable, for long after that event, the Kardamaka and Kṣaharātas, pushed out by Darius, started their śakakāla beginning in 550 B.C. with their ouster or settlement in India.[65] Be what it may, it seems certain that the Hebrews were the migrating Ābhiras from India.

Thus far we have endeavoured to show how the refugees, fleeing before the watery fury of the floods in the Sarasvatī valley traversed the whole of west Asian territories and managed to reach its farthest limits. Now, hereafter we will try to trace their *passover* from Asia to Africa till they reached its central and southern regions.

These refugees, owing to the circumscribing circumstances, were largely unable to retrieve their other valuables save the herds of cattle. Again, as they were moving through already well-settled lands, they were unable to find suitable agricultural land to settle down and had, perforce, to survive only as cowherds. As against the agriculturists who are firmly bound to their land and fertile fields, the cowherds have no such compunction and are always free to move on or about in search of pastures afresh and if ethnic comparisons have any value in assessing the historical truths, it is not unlikely that Indian herders, bypassing or even traversing the well-settled Egypt, had managed somehow to reach as far as central and even southern Africa.

African cowherds are reported to have believed that their forefathers

> 'had their origins far to the north (and east), along some mythical valley, a place they called the Beginning of All Things'.
>
> 'Generations before, their tribe had been overtaken by some cataclysmic events, another *mefecane* (a great slaughter 'the pounding of the tribes, like corn between the grinding stones of the impis) and the famine that naturally followed. They and their herds had begun the long migration (west and) southwards plundering and killing all the other tribes that stood in their path. As pastorlists and nomads they always moved on seeking grazing for their herds, more plunder and women----'[66]

This summary description of the lifestyle of the migrant forefathers of the African cowherds brings at once to mind that of the Vrātyas, the degenerate Kṣatriyas as delineated in *Atharva Veda*. It is said that while they were standing tall in the east, all the gods, i.e., the learned and the officials followed them in their big chariots' [67] when, however, they migrated west, they had lost their kingdom and, once impoverished, they became shabby and disfigured. And when they reached south they had only the cattle as their sole possession and faithful followers.[69] In yet another *sūkta* it is said that no one dared to kill them or their cattle.[70] And wherever they arrived, they were accorded the welcome due to an honoured guest, lest the territory was ravaged and the people ravished.[71] Thus propitiated the dreaded Vrātya cowherds moved on at their own accord.[72]

Their cattle were of heavy build, with prominent and heavy hump and swinging dewlap. Their long and pointed horns spread wide. These cattle were much prized if only for their ability to defend themselves against the lions and other predatory beasts.[73] Such a heavy breed of cattle with long and pointed and wide spreading horns is still favoured and found especially in Saurashtra in western India.

Their settlements where the chiefs resided, was "laid out in an enormous circle, divided internally into rings within rings like an archery target" called *Kraal* in 'Afrikaans', it was "surrounded by a high stockade, and at its heart was a vast cattle pen, in which all the royal herd could be contained". The king liked to live close to his beasts" and it was explained "how the inner enclosure also served as a fly-trap. The insects laid their eggs in the fresh cattle-dung where they were trodden under the hoofs of the milling herd and could not hatch".

"The outer circles" of the 'Kraal' "were filled with the closely spaced beehive huts" that housed the king and his close associates and their families. "All these huts were, however, dwarfed by the king's 'palace', --- it did not seem possible that sticks and reeds could have been built up so high without collapsing ---. It looked like the egg of the *roe*".[74]

The above description of the royal seat recalls the layout of the 'ash-mounds' as exposed and reconstructed by a host of archaeologists since 1957. These ash-mounds have been identified in the Krishna-Tungabhadra valley in the lower and in the Tapi basin in the upper Deccan plateau.[75] Though once such royal settlements must have dotted the whole of northern plains, the density of population and the recurring floods in the Sindhu-Gaṅgā plains must certainly have either pulverized or washed them out of existence. In Saurashtra they have either been pulverised or washed out of existence. In Saurashtra and Maharasthra, in the post-draught period, the cattle keeper's settlements-*gawali than-* abound, but' like every other material remains, the chiefs vanish and only the impoverished cattle-keepers somehow managed to survive.

Again, when the king or chief died, he was interned in a crosslegged sitting posture-*padmāsana* or lotuspose-into a deep pit and his personal belongings including his favourite pots and weapons as also the royal insignia were buried along with him.[76] This, too, is reminiscent of disposal of the dead body of saints, perhaps of the gosain-*gosvāmin,* literally the 'cattle ownerssect's.

Be what it may, these African cowherds have huge herds, and 'love their' cattle like their own children. They do not slaughter them to eat their meat. In times of necessity such as locust-caused famine, instead they tap off their blood, a practice they must have learnt during their long sojourn in west Asia, and mix it with the milk.[77] That becomes their main food.

Since childhood the boys were sent to the far-flung cow-pens, which served also, very much like the *gurukulas*[78] of India, as schools prepatory to manhood. Here they mastered not only the science of cattle-keeping but also came to recognize "each animal by name, which bull covered their dames, ... each one's age and temper .... the remedy and the treatment for every disease to which the herds are prone" and fought off the "lions who were attacking the animals".[79] While living in these cattle-pen cum *gurukula* like residential schools, they also learnt and mastered under the expert tutelage of the elders the use of all sorts of weapons and missiles and became adept in the science of individual combat as well as mass attack.

These cowherds move from one pasturage to another along their large herds. During such movements, the cowherds stalked along the left and right of the herd, while the bulk of them formed the 'drag'. They were all wrapped in their leather cloak and held their *assegai* in their hand and slung their black war shields on their back. The 'point man', usually the chief-herder played on a reed-flute, as he went, a sweet but monotonous tune and the cattle followed him like faithful hounds. The wagon train brought up the rear-guard. The cattles moved and spread out like a river in flood across the wild. By the time the entire herd was on the move they covered several leagues.[80]

"These warriors are big men built like iron-wood trees. They wear black vulture feathers in their head-dress. They have rattles on their wrists and ankles so their legions make the sound of wind when they come", which demoralizes the enemy. They carry black shields of dried ox-hide and instead of throwing javelins, they prefer to come close with their short stabbing *assegai*. The wound from that blade is so wide and deep that it sucks the blood from the victim like a river as they pluck out the steel.[81]

Here again we must hark back to the Vedic account of the *Vrātyas*. In one *mantra* they are said to look blue black if looked from the front and red from behind.[82] It is, therefore, not unlikely that the wooden handles of these *assigai* had turned black from firehardening, while their shields of raw hide were either naturally red or painted. During the fight they rounded their enemies with the black wooden handles and only pierced the resisting ones with their iron/bronzed tips.[83]

Their main entertainment was their traditional war dance. In it a few danced while the rest surrounded them and watched. After sometime the dancers retired and joined the onlookers and a new set of dancers took the floor and the show continued. During such dances, while the reed flute and rattles too had their significant role to play, the major congruity that I want to point out was that during the dance the participants often took a high leap and when they came down, they struck the earth with one foot, and ended their song with a long-drawn and loud '*jee ee ee*' refrain, in which the onlookers too joined.[84]

This short description of perhaps their only entertainment serves sufficient food for thought and comparison. During the days of our childhood, living as we did on the edge of the Faizabad city, we had numerous occasions to witness the traditional dance of the non-urbanised *Ahirs*-cowherds. In this dance, in which women seldom participated, the men wore dhotis above which was drawn a pair of tight knickers made out of multi-coloured pieces of cloth stitched together. They were also embellished along the waist and both the thighs with rattles.Their torso was left naked but for a black upper garment round their necks, the two ends of which hung loose near the knees. In their hands, the dancers carried a reed flute. Their dance started with the playing of the flute and during the dance they performed high leaps and, like their African counterparts, they struck the earth with one, usually the right, foot and shouted their battle cry '*jee ee ee*'. During my working days, too, a similar performance, with, however, a different dress was on many occasions seen in Mahoba, UP., as well.[85]

Though only a few and far between, these similarities between the two far away communities from India and Africa, seem to suggest that the African cowherds are only the descendants of the refugees from India, that migrated soon after the start of the *Dvāpara* age, owing to cataclysm in the Sarasvatī valley.[86]

The descendants of these Kṣatriya refugees, though well educated themselves, soon lost their education and culture due to the loss of contact with the learned Brāhmaṇa teachers and became *Vṛsala-Vrātya*.[87] And when after the long trek they reached Africa, they had retained only their cattle and a joint memory of the land called "the Beginning of All Things". Here it would perhaps not be out of place to mention that Manu mentions one such people as "jhalla",[88] which sounds quite like, and, therefore, reminds one of the Julus of South Africa. That this equation is not wholly preposterous seems to be suggested by the evidence of a medieval Muslim history "*Gulshan-i'Ibrahim*", popularly known as *Tarikh-i-Ferishta*. The author, writing on the basis of various earlier records, states that long before the advent of Mohammad, the founder of Islam, the Indian Brāhmīns used to visit and worship the numerous idols at the temple of Kaba and the priests from Kaba, called "*Al-Hum*" reciprocated by visiting and worshipping at Somanatha,[89] on the Arabian coast of Saurasthtra. It is perhaps these very "*Al-Hum*" priests from Kaba who are mentioned by Manu as the *Brāhmaṇa Vrātya* named *Saikha*.[90]

In the light of what has been said above, we would not be far wrong to say that the Indian migrants, too, helped to populate the Central and South Africa, long before the Europeans reached there and tried to exterminate the African people and failing which did their best to wipe out their traditional lifestyle, i.e. the culture.

References

1. बृहस्पते प्रथम वाचो अग्र यत्प्रैरत नामधेयं दधानाः।
   यदेषा श्रेष्ठं यदरिप्रमासीत्प्रेणा तंदेषां निहितं गुहाविः ।। ऋग्वेद (ऋ.) 10.71.1.
2. एष श्लोकोऽभ्युक्तो–
   ये समुद्रान्निरखनन्देवास्तीक्ष्णेभिरभ्रिभिः।
   सुदेवोऽअद्य तद्विद्याद्यत्र निर्वपणं दधुः।। इति, शतपथ ब्राह्मण (श.ब्रा.) 7.5.2.52

3. ते वै सर्वे तूपरा भवन्ति। पुरुषो वै प्रजापतेर्नेदिष्टं सोऽयं तूपरोऽविषाण:। ....।। *श.ब्रा.* 5.1.3.8; 5.2.1.6.
4. पुरुष ह वै देवा:। अग्रे पशुमालेभिरे तस्यालब्धस्य अश्वमालभन्त गामालभन्त अविमालभन्त अजमालभन्त .... *श.ब्रा.* 1.2.3.6; पुरुषं प्रथममालभते। पुरुषो हि प्रथम: पशूनाम–वहीं 6.2.1.18 **ऐतरेय ब्राह्मण** (*ऐ. ब्रा.*) 2.6.7. तैत्तिरीय ब्राह्मण (तै.ब्रा.) 3.9.8.2–3 इत्यादि।
5. इमं पशुं पशुपते ते अद्य बध्नाम्यग्ने सुकृतस्य मध्ये।
अनु मन्यस्व सुयजा यजाम जुष्टं देवानामिदमस्तु हव्यन्।। तैत्तिरीय संहिता (तै.सं) 3.1.4.2.
6. येषामीशे पशुपति: पशूनां चतुष्पदामुत च द्विपदाम्
निष्क्रीतोऽयं यज्ञियं भागमेतु रायस्पोषा यजमानस्य सन्तु।। वही 4.
7. य आरण्या: पशवो विश्वरूपा विरूपा: सन्तो बहुधैकरूपा:।
वायुस्तां अग्रे प्र मुमोत्तु देव: प्रजापति: प्रजया संविदान:।। वही 6.
8. जीवं देवानामप्येतु पाथ: सत्या: सन्तु यजमानस्य कामा:। वही 8.
9. घृतेन त्वं तनुवो वर्धयस्व स्वाहाकृतं हविरदन्तु देवा:।। वही 14.
10. य ईशे पशुपति: पशूनां चतुष्पदामुत यो द्विपदाम्।
निष्क्रीत: स यज्ञियं भागमेतु रायस्पोषा यजमानं सचन्ताम्।। अथर्ववेद (*अ.वे.*)2.34.1.
11. ऋ.वे. 1.179.5.
12. अरुणकुमार, *देवयान संस्कृति का विकास और वेद*, फैजाबाद 1996.
13. S.H. Hooke, *Middle Eastern Mythology*, Pelican Books, 1963, pp. 29, 45
14. अरुणकुमार, *इतिहास की भारतीय परम्परा और पुरातत्व*, प्रकाशनाधीन
15. ऋ.वे. 7.18.5; अरुणकुमार, *'इतिहास'* इत्यादि, पृ. 106–110.
16. पञ्चनद्य: सरस्वतीमपि यन्ति सस्रोतस:।
सरस्वती तु पञ्चधा सो देशेऽभवत्सरित्।। *यजुर्वेद* (य.वे.) 34.11.
17. डा॰ रामविलास शर्मा, *भारत के प्राचीन भाषा परिवार और हिन्दी*, तीन खण्ड, दिल्ली, 1179–1981.
18. डा॰ रामविलास शर्मा, *पश्चिमी एशिया और ऋग्वेद*, दिल्ली 1994.
19. Hooke, S.H., *op, cit., p. 31*
20. Pritchard, J.B., *The Ancient Near Eastern Texts Relating to the old Testament*, Princeton 1950, p. 44.
21. Hooke, *op cit.*, p. 136.
22. *Ibid.*, pp. 47-49.
31. S.N. Kramer, Dilmun: Quest for Paradise, *Antiquity*, Vol. 37, 1963, pp. 111-115; Arun Kumar, On the Location of Dilmun, *Journal of the Oriental Institute*, Baroda, Vol. xxi, Nos. 1-4; अरुणकुमार, *इतिहास* etc, पृ. 140–143.
32. अरुणकुमार, वही पृ. 54–58, 61–65.
33. वही, पृ. 124; Possehl, G.L. *Indus Age, The Beginnings*, Delhi-1999, pp. 453, 462-64, 466.

34. Hooke, *op. cit.*, p. 22.
35. *Ibid*, pp. 72-73.
36. प्रजापतिः प्रजा असृजत सोऽरिच्यत-ताण्ड्य ब्राह्मण (ता.ब्रा.) 8.10.1;
    प्रजापतिः प्रजाः सृष्ट्वा वृत्तोऽशयत्-तै.ब्रा. 1.2.6.1.
37. Hooke, *op cit,* 95.
38. O.R. Gurney, *The Hittites,* Pelican Book, pp. 1o4-105
39. वही, पृ. 215.
40. वही, पृ. 181-82; Hooke, *op. cit.*,p. 96-98.
41. अधा शयीत निर्ऋतेरुपस्थेऽधैनं वृका रभसासो अद्युः।। ऋ. वे. 10.95.14.
42. पुरूरवो मा मृथा मा प्र पप्तो मा त्वो वृकासो अशिवास उक्षन् ।
    न वै स्त्रैणानि संख्यानि सन्ति सालावृकाणां हृदयान्येता।। वही, मं. 15
43. Gurney, *op. cit.*,pp. 184-188.
44. Bhuvan Vikrama and Arun Kumar, "The collapse of the Sarasvata Sabhyata : An Elegy in Mahābhārata" in *Puraratna,*(Ed.) C. Margabandhu *et.al.,* Delhi 2002, pp. 86-96
45. Gurney, *op. cit.,* pp. 187.
46. *ibid.*,pp. 188-189.
47. *Bible, Genesis* 2.18.
48. Hook, *op. cit.*,pp. 112-113.
49. *Bible, Ezekiel,* 20-12-19.
50. *Bible, Job,* 15.7-8.
51. अरुणकुमार, *इतिहास* .... पृ. 57-58
52. वही, पृ. 115-119, 130-135
53. Bhuvana Vikrama and Arun Kumar, *op.cit.*
54. Weiss, H., *et.al.* "The Genesis and Collapse of the Third Millennium North Mesopotamian Civilisation", Science 1993, 261, pp. 995-1004.
55. Courty, Mary Agnes, "Spatial and Temporal Dynamics of the Late Third Millennium Abrupt Changes and Socio-economic Collapse: Problem, Evidence, Scepticism and More Questions", paper presented at the *3rd Archaeology Congress,* New Delhi-2002.
56. Hooke, *op. cit.,* p. 141.
57. ibid., p. 79.
58. रामविलास शर्मा, वही, खण्ड 3, 1981, पृ. 71.
59. Hooke, *op. cit.,* pp. 121-126.

60. *Bible,* Judges, 4.11-17.
61. Hook, *op. cit.,*p. 127.
62. Alfred Guillaume, *Islam,* Pelican Book, 1964, p. 2.
63. K.M. Munshi, *Glory that was Gurjardesa,* Mumbai 1965, p. 168.
64. ताण्ड्य ब्राह्मण, 25.10.6; कात्यायन श्रौतसूत्र 24.5.30 etc.
65. K.D. Sethna, *Ancient India in a New Light,* Delhi 1989, pp. 463-64; पं. उदयवीर शास्त्री, *आचार्य शंकर का काल,* दिल्ली 1991.
66. Willbur Smith, *The Blue Horizon* (a novel), 2003, pp. 341, cf. 291.
67. स उदतिष्ठत् स प्राची दिशमनुव्यचलत्। तं बृहच्च रथन्तरं चादित्याश्च विश्वे च देवा अनुव्यचलन्-अ.वे. 15.2.1-2
68. त वैरूपं च वैराज च .... अनुव्यचलन्-वही, 15.2.
69. स दक्षिणां दिशमनुव्यचलत्। तं ..... पशवश्चानुव्यचलन्-वही, 15.2.
70. नास्य पशन् न समानाम् हिनस्ति-वही, 15.5.3-16.
71. तद् यस्यैवं ..... व्रात्यो राज्ञोतिथिर्गृहानागच्छेत्। श्रेयांसमेनमात्मनो मानयेत, तथा क्षत्राय ना वृश्चते तथा राष्ट्राय ना वृश्चते-वही, 15.10.11-12.
72. ऐन निकामो गच्छति-वही, 15.11.11
73. Wilbur Smith, *op. cit.,* p. 492.
74. *Ibid.,* pp. 584-585.
75. A. Ghosh (Ed.) *An Encyclopaedia of Indian Archaeology,* Vol. I, Delhi 1989, Munshi Ram Manohar Lal, pp. 103, 293.
76. Wilbur Smith. *The Sparrow Falls* (a noval), p. 402.
77. Wilbur Smith. *The Blue Horizon,* p. 303.
78. तम् (सत्यकाम् जावालं) उपनीय कृशानामवलानं चतुःशता गा निराकृत्योवाचेमाः सोम्याऽनुसं व्रजेति।। ताअभिप्रस्थापयन्नुवाच नाऽसहस्त्रेणाऽऽवर्तयेति- *छांदोग्य* उप. 4.5.5.
79. Cf. Kālidāsa's *Raghuvamsa* where Raghu is reported to have offered his own body in lieu of the cow Nandini, whom a lion had captured.
80. Wilbut Smith, *The Blue Horizon,* p. 340; वाश्रा इव धेनवः स्यन्दमाना अञ्जः समुद्रमव जग्मुरापः।- ऋ. वे. 1.32.2.
81. *Ibid.,* p. 291.
82. नीलमस्योदरं लोहितं पृष्ठम्-अ.वे. 15.1.7.
83. नीलेनैवाप्रियं भ्रातृव्यं प्रोर्णोति लोहितेन द्विषन्तं विध्यतीति-वही, 15.1.8.
84. Wilbur Smith, *The Angles Weep* (a novel), p. 142.
85. For a description of the song and the refrain, see डॉ. शिवप्रसाद सिंह, कुहरे में युद्ध (उपन्यास).

86. डॉ. अरुणकुमार, *इतिहास की भारतीय परम्परा और पुरातत्व*, प्रकाशनाधीन.

87. शनकैस्तु क्रियालोपादिमाः क्षत्रिय जातयः।
वृषलत्वं गता लोके ब्राह्मणादर्शनेन च।। *मनुस्मृति* 10.43.

88. भल्लो .... राजन्याद व्रात्याद etc., वही, 10.22

89. Farishta, M.Q., *Tarikh,* Translated by John Brigges, *History of the Rise and Fall* of *The Mohammedan Power in India till the Year A.D. 1612*. London, 1929, Vol. IV, p. 402, n.

90. व्रात्यातु जायते विप्रात् ...... शैख एव च, *मनुस्मृति* 10.21.

3

Palaeobotanical Remains of Wheat and Barley : As Revealed in Archaeological Excavations in India

*—Pushp Lata Singh**

Ṛg Veda[1] mentioned wheat and barley as *Yava* which appears to be a generic term for any sort of 'grain' and not merely 'barley' . On latter text as in the *Atharva Veda*[2], it is more frequent. According to *Kauṣitaki Brāhmaṇa*[3] and Taittirya Saṁhitā[4], the barely harvest came after spring in the summer. That barely was cultivated in the period of the *Ṛg Veda*[5] is not certain but its probability cannot be ignored[6]. So, far as '*Go Duma*' (wheat) is concerned, is frequently referred to be plural in the *Yajur Veda Saṁhitā*[7] and *Brāhmaṇas*[8] and is expressly distinguished from 'rice' (*vrihi*) or 'barely' (*yava*)[9]. Groats (*saktavah*) made by this grain are also mentioned[10]. The word occurs in the singular in the '*Śatapatha Brāhmaṇa*'[11]. There were two harvests (sasya) a year according to the *Taittiriya Saṁhitā,* the winter crop was ripe in the month of Chaitra (March-April) according to the *Kauṣitaki Brāhmaṇa.*

Archaeologically, the antiquity of cultivation of barely and wheat outside India goes back to the Neolithic period. At Jerico (Jordan) two row hulled barely and emmer wheat was found in Aceramic Neolithic levels dated to *circa* 8350 B.C.- *circa* 7350 B.C. Barely was at Beudha, Alikosh, Hacilar in western Asia at the beginning of the seventh millennium B.C., while at Jarmo (Iraq) and Tepe Guran in the Zagros region (*circa* 6000 B.C.), Catal Hayuk (Turkey) *circa* 6000 B.C. has produced emmer, einkorn, bread wheat and six row naked barely. Such domesticated varieties have been reported from Mesopotamian Neolithic strata in *circa* 5000 B.C.[12]

---

* Senior Lecturer in Environmental Archaeology, Department of History, Culture and Archaeology, Dr. Ram Manohar Lohia Avadh University, Faizabad-224001.

Archaeology has traced the process of wheat and barley domestication in Indian subcontinent at Mehargarh (in Baluchistan) where it has been found in both cultivated and wild forms which shows a local process of domestication. In the *Aceramic-Neolithic* period (I) the following varieties of wheat and barely occur :[13]

Wheat (*Triticum*)	—	*Triticum monococcum*
	—	*Triticum dicoccum*
	—	*Triticum durum* and
	—	*Triticum* sp.

Only small amounts of these varieties are present, but the presence of einkorn, emmer and bread or durum wheat is as J.F. Jarrige points out interesting because "wild wheats are not known from this part of the Middle East today.[14]

Barely (Hordeum)	—	*Hordeum distichum*
	—	*Hordeum spontaneum*
	—	*Hordeum vulgare varudum*
	—	*Hordeum sphaerococcum*
	—	*Hordeum* sp.

H. *vulgare var. nudum* constituting 91% of the total cereal finds of the period. It has also been surmised that at first the naked six-row barely (*H. vulgare var nudum*) were "perhaps not completely domesticated" *H. spontaneum* is absent after period I. *H. distichum* occurs only in Pd I and period III. A study of 30 bricks on large fragments produced 5956 identified impressions. The proportions of the various texa are : 91% six row barely, 4% einkorn, emmer, 2.5% wild barely and 0.7% durum bread wheat. The study revealed that naked six row barely was the principal crop to supply the straw used to make mud bricks during the Aceramic Neolithic at Mehargarh. The hulled wheat of period I had undergone an intensive process of cultivation and domestication while wheat and barley were the principal crops at Mehargarh[15] in Pakistan.

In the ceramic Neolithic period II at Mehargarh *Triticum monococcum* (einkorn), *Tricum dicoccum* (emmer) and *T. durum* (durum or bread wheat) continue to occur, but side by side there is the presence of *Triticum aestivum, Triticum compactum* and *Triticum sphaerococcum.* These are among the modern varieties of wheat and most frequent at the later protohistoric sites of the Subcontinent including the Indus

Civilization sites. The fact that the forms like einkorn, emmer and durum/bread wheat occur earlier in the sequence in relation to these staple and persistent varieties is a clear indication of the local domestication of wheat in the Mehargarh region.

At Gufkral in Jammu and Kashmir (Aceramic Neolithic-pre 2100 B.C.) barley (*Java*) *Hordeum vulgare* linn, six row barley-*var hexastichum* and wheat[16] (*Triticum aestivum*) have been reported. The ceramic Neolithic (*circa* 2100 B.C.) also give the evidence of wheat (*Triticum*) and barley (*Hordeum vulgare* Linn). On the basis of the above evidence it has been suggested by Kajale[17] that at the site the cultivation of barely and wheat is prior to that of rice (which constitutes staple cereal diet of the Kashmiries today). Burzahomians of Neolithic period also cultivated wheat and barely in the early centuries of the second millennium B.C.

In the Vindhyan region of India, Mahagara[18] has yielded an interesting and important evidence of domesticated barley from Neolithic period. Two carbonized grains from Neolithic horizon of the site (locus XXXVI-XXXVII), erosional pit-1, depth 2.60-2.77 m) have been on examination referred to as barley[19] (*Hordeum vulgare*). Although this region was suitable for the rice based cultivation.

In the Gangetic Valley the earliest occurrence of wheat and barley is reported from Chirand. According to Vishnu-Mittre[20] the depth at which wheat grains have been found at this site is much below the depth on which C14 date is reported which is 1755 B.C. radio-carbon and his own estimate of the beginning of occupation of Chirand is *C.* 3500 B.C. Even if one is reluctant to admit of such high antiquity, *circa.* 2500 B.C. seems to be a reasonable enough inference. The plant remains recovered from Layer 17 of C.RD XI[21] (Neolithic level) includes wheat (*Triticum sphaerococcum*) along with rice and other cereals. The single kernel of wheat is short, oblong, grooved and thick with the ends broad and blunt. It measures 3.75 mm long' 2.75 mm broad and 1.75mm thick. The dorsal surface of the grain is domed and the groove is deep. In the lessar L/B h/T, and higher B/L and T/L indicates that it further compares with the indices of grains *T. sphaerococcum.*

Barley was represented by thirteen grains most of which are naked. These thirteen grains are very much worn out measuring about 4.5 ×2.25-3.25 ×1.50 mm -2.25 mm. Most of them are naked since the pales are absent and the surface bears rippling marks. The grains are evenly rounded in cross section apart from the ventral furrow which is shallow with a soft longitudinal depression on the dorsal side. Some grains show slight deviation from the straight shape suggesting that the spike was six row and probably of the nodding type, a *Hordeum* sp. The grains longitudinal stripping arising from the remains of the pales or from the longitudinal surface cells of the seed coat[22]. The cross section of these grains is not angular. These might have belonged to the hulled barley. The measurement of six random grains are given below :

Measurement of Random Chirand Grains of Barley

	L	*B*	*T*
	4.00	2.50	1.75
	4.25	2.75	2.00
	4.80	2.80	2.25
	5.00	3.00	1.75
	5.00	3.25	1.50
	5.25	2.25	1.70
Average	4.17	2.28	1.70

The data from Chirand has been supplemented by Senuwar excavation (1986-87 and 1989-90) : located in vicinity of Kaimur ranges about 10 km. S.W. of Sasaram in Bihar. The earliest sub period I A termed, Pure Neolithic' has yielded barley (*Hordeuym vulgare*) dwarf wheat (*Triticum shaerococcum*). In the sub period IB (Neolithic-Chalcolithic and with a radio carbon date of 1770 ±120 B.C.) the carbonized grains comprise barley (*Hordeum vulgare*), two forms of wheat viz., dwarf-wheat (*Triticum sphaerococcum*) and bread wheat (*T. aestivum*).[23]

In the Saryupar region Imlidih (Gorakhpur) was another site, located about 30 km to the west of Narhan. Its Pd I of cord impressed Red Ware culture (Pre 1300 B.C.) has yielded[24] remains of wheat and barley along with rice. Thirty two grains were found and their general features confirm with those of bread wheat (*Triticum sphaerococcum*). Whole or fragmentary grains of hulled and six row barley (*Hordeum vulgare*) in the mixed samples, are frequently met with.

Early Harappan :

Early Harappan phase at Mehargarh period III witnessed even greater diversification[25] in agriculture then was the case during period II. Wheat is indicated only by *Triticum* sp. and variety of *H. distichum* occurs only in period III. No wheat is reported in period IV but *H. sphaerococcum* (Barley) is present. In period V and VI there are *T. discoccum, T. aestivum. T. compactum. T. sphaerococcum and Triticum* sp. *H. Vulgare* is recorded in period V-VIII but *H. vulgare var. nudum* is absent in period IV which shows no remains at all but is present in the other periods. *H. sphaerococcum* does not occur in period III but is present in the other periods. Wheat is also reported from period VII and VIII both yield *T. aestivum, T. compoactum, T. sphaerococcum* and *Triticum* sp.[26] This brings us to the close of the third millennium B.C. which has started around 7000 B.C. in the area of Baluchistan.

The first cereal remains identified at Mundigak come from period II (*circa*. 3500 B.C.) and they include domesticated[27] wheat (*T. compoactum*). At Balakot the grains of *Hordeum vulgare* (six row barley) is present in Early Harappan level (between 4000 B.C. and 2900 B.C.). *H. vulgare var. nudum* figures in the early Harappan Tarakai Qila assemblage in the Bannu area in the third millennium B.C. or possibly a little earlier[28]. *Triticum sp*. also occurs in the early Harappan Kot Diji context at Tarakai Qila, Ninduri in South Baluchistan has *T. aestivum* in the Kulli context of the third millennium B.C.[29]

It is pertinent to point out here that the Early Harappans on this side of the Indo-Pakistan border are much later than Early-Harappans on the lower status. In India at Rohira in district Sangrur cereals comprised of remains wheat (*T. Sphaerococcum*) and emmer wheat, (*T. dicoccum*). The five complete kernels of barley (*H. vulgare*, three elongated kernels of emmer wheat, three carbonized grains of Indian dwarf wheat were reported.[30]

Harappan :

In Harappan context wheat and barley occur at Harappa, Mohenjodaro, Chanhudaro, Kalibangan, Banawali and Rohira. Harappan carbonized remains of wheat partly lumped together and partly scattered were recovered from two places. One was found in Mound in great granary area. These grains were identified by J.C. Luthra as grains of *Triticum compactum* (dwarf wheat) still cultivated in Punjab. B.C. Burt identified these grains as those of *Triticum sphaerococcum perc*.

The other specimen of wheat was found in a trench at the southern edge of mound AB in association with stratum II.[31] These were also identified as those of *Triticum*. Besides, a small quantity of charred barley was recovered from mound AB stratum III. Luthra identified them as common husked but Burt identified it as *Hordeum vulgare L. var hexastichum* (six row barley).

At Mohenjodro large quantity of wheat was found lying on a pavement of a later date in L. Area.[32] These grains were identified as club wheat (*Triticum compactum*) or (*Triticum sphaerococcum*). Samples of barley found from the H.R. area were identified by Percival as *Hordeum vulgare*[33]. According to Vishnu Mittre and R. Savithri, Harappans of Mohenjodro and Chanhudaro were growing *Triticum sphaerococcum*, *Triticum aestivum* and *Triticum compactum*. Mohenjodro produced only one broken hulled grain of barley whereas Chanhudaro yielded two barley hulled and ten naked grains of barley[34].

Kalibangan period II was identified by mature Harappan culture albeit the Early Harappan also lived together for some time though in small number. Kalibagan Harappan people produced wheat and barley along with other crops[35]. Samples collected from the smaller mound were found to contain several thousand charred grains of hulled barley, 50 grains of naked barley. The barley cultivated by Harappans at Kalibangan were of the variety of hulled grains[36]. The naked barley was less common as revealed by a few naked grains. The grains of wheat is *Triticum sphaerococcum*. These grains possess characteristics intermediate between wheat and barley.

Late Harappan :

Late Harappan site of Hulas in upper Gaṅgā plain has yielded *Hordeum vulgare, Triticum sphaerococcum* and *Triticum compactum*[37]. These palaeobotanical remains show that Harappans entered the rice cultivation area as the progenitors of rice are known to occur in wild form in marshes and riverine habitats in the Gaṅgā Plains. Dikshit is of the view that both its domestication and diffusion must have involved the human movement and cultural interaction[38] of Mahorana in Ludhiana. The carbonized food grains trench MRN-42 V ×41 period IB dating from *circa* 2100 B.C.-*circa* 1900 B.C. have been referred to as hulled and naked six row barley (*Hordeum vulgare* L. and *H. vulgare L. var nudum*), club wheat (*Triticum compactum*) etc.[39]

The remains of barley and wheat are also reported from Rohira in District Sangrur in Punjab. Its period IB dating back from *circa* 2000-*circa* 1700 B.C. comprised of two forms of barley hulled (*Hordeum vulgare L. emened Biwden*) and naked (*H. vulgare L. var nudum*), two forms of wheat, short wheat (*T. sphaerococcum perc.*) and some grains tentatively regarded as aberrant-ones, but resembling with the peculiar kernels of glumed wheat (*Triticum dococcum*) etc.

Chalcolithic Culture of Deccan :

The site of Kaytha at Ujjain (Kaytha culture, *circa* 2000-1800 B.C.) brought out two kinds[40] of wheat (*Triticum sphaerococcum* and *Triticum compactum*) while Malwa culture (1700-1250) has yielded remains of wheat and barley in phases II and IV at Navadatoli. The botanical remains have been reported from Jorwe culture (1400-700 B.C.) at Inamgaon (Dist. Pune), Diambad (Dist. Ahmadnagar) and Sonegaon. At Inamgaon the people of Malwa and Jorwe culture cultivated barley and wheat with other cereals[41]. The presence of barley (66 complete grains) at Inamgaon during the Malwa culture is intriguing in so far as it is not known from other sites where this culture has been discovered. Dhavalikar is of the opinion that the black cotton soil was the prime single factor. The hard, compact, black soil is known for its fertility and moisture retaining capacity, it is capable of yielding rich harvest[42] if cultivated effectively. But according to Agrawal Chalcolithic agriculture was generally confined to alluvial patches only and the black cotton soil could not have been cultivated[43]. However, it is pertinent to point here that there are no alluvial stretches along the Deccan rivers which run through hilly uplands, and they do not deposit the fertilizing silt on their banks like the rivers of the Indo Gangetic plains. The rivers in the Deccan flow through rocky uplands and have no alluvial strips worth the name along their banks. Dhavalikar estimated the population of Inamgaon to be about a thousand persons and showed that at least 800 hectare of arable[44] land was required for them. This much soil is not available and therefore black soil had to be cultivated. He suggests that perhaps wooden ploughs were used to cultivate the black soil[45].

Inamgaon has shown that the early Jorwe farmers cultivated two crops[46] a year, Kharif and Rabi as at present. The Jorwe people cultivated barley, wheat, sorghum, lentil and occasionally rice. Barley was the dominant crop right from Malwa to late Jorwe period. It seems that barley cultivation was preferred to wheat since the frequency of barley is 21 times that of wheat. The reason behind this was the climate of the region. Barley is a crop of short duration and can be raised without difficulty in a semi arid climate. Wheat was the next important crop. Dhavalikar had the opinion that although the peasents of the Malwa cultivated wheat in Malwa, they do not seem to have cultivated it in the Deccan because this cereal has not been reported from the Malwa levels of any Chalcolithic site in the Deccan. According to him wheat is a rabi crop which required winter rain. The semi arid climate of the Deccan does not receive winter rains and consequently wheat could not have been grown by the people of the Malwa culture in Deccan. The Jorwe farmers of Inamgaon could grow this cereal because of adequate water supply which was stored in the channels dug along the embankment which they had constructed to divert the flood water of the Ghod river. This massive embankment was about 240m long and 2.25 m wide and perhaps equally high which indicates a higher rainfall and frequent floods. This embankment[47] was built to divert flood water through a channel which was sufficiently deep (2.50m) and wide (4m) and about 200m long. This channel was also used for irrigating fields nearby. Consequently rice was cultivated[48]. The first appearance[49] of rice was seen in the 5th layer of trenches C6 and D4. The presence of rice need not necessarily indicate rice cultivation around the site. The Chalcolithic habitants might have brought it to the site from upstream regions of Ghod river where the region received higher rainfall (above 750mm) and topographical conditions were suitable for its natural and proper growth.

During Late Jorwe phase (Pd III) *circa* 1000 B.C.-*circa* 700 B.C. at Inamgaon, the said irrigation channel was choked by silt. This was due to climatic fluctuation (dry). This drastic climate change look place around *circa* 1000 B.C. Climate became more arid. The chalcolithic settlements were not deserted and continued to survive in a poor state. Their poverty is reflected in their small round huts, coarse pottery and the decline in agriculture[50].

Besides Inamgaon, Daimabad has furnished evidence of earliest agriculture[51] in chalcolithic culture of the Deccan. Phase I of Savalda culture (*circa* 2200-2000 B.C.) people cultivated wheat and barley. From the buff and cream ware phase of Diamabad wheat and barley were recordered. Phase IV of Malwa culture yielded carbonized grains of wheat (*Triticum sphaerococcum, Triticum compactum*), barley (*Hordeum sp.*) along with other cereals. The grains of wheat (165-173) out number those of barley (35-36) in both Malwa and Jorwe phases. It is essential to mention here that comparatively the Jorwe samples are rich in number of grains than those of the Malwa samples. However the food economy in both was largely alike but for some differences wheat, barley elusine, peas, pulses etc. are common ones.[53] The wheat occurs only from Malwa and Jorwe levels while this cereal is significantly absent in the earlier three phases, barley was the staple food of this region as it is present in all the five phases at Diamabad.

The samples of charred grains of Sonegaon[54] of Early Jorwe phase was obtained from the debris of a burnt wall, at a depth of about 2m below the datum line. This sample shows that it contained 120 grains of barely (*Hordeum vulgare Linn.*) preserved in an excellent condition. The average shape and size of the grains indicate that these were the cultivated variety. All these grains show transverse rippling on both the dorsal and ventral surfaces, an indirect evidence of the husked nature of the grains. The evidence of barley has come from other chalcolithic sites of the Deccan such as Navadatoli and Inamgaon. Carbonized[55] material from Sonegaon consisted of charred kernels of wheat indentified as *Triticum sphaerococcum.*

Ochre Coloured Pottery Culture :

The inhabitants of the O.C.P. culture of Atranjikhera[56] and Sringverpur cultivated wheat and barley along with other cereals. The inhabitants of Atranjikhera during the O.C.P. period grew two crops in a year, one in the summer and the other in winter. They cultivated rice in summer which needs plenty of water for its proper growth and cultivated barley which is a well known winter crop. The Vedic literature has emphasized rotation of crops in order to maintain soil fertility and crop productivity. It has been suggested on the basis of Atranjikhera evidence[57] that perhaps the OCP people initiated the rotation of crops even earlier to the Vedic period.

The evidence of remains of barley and rice are represented by several grains[58] at Sringverpur. Although the north eastern and eastern part of India is the ancestral land of rice, barley is of west Asian origin. Barley is common cereal of Harappans. So the introduction and spread of barley beyond eastern borders of Harappan culture should indeed be attributed to the of Harappans.

Black and Red Ware Culture :

The people of Black and Red Ware culture of Atranjikhera[59] in upper Gangetic plain cultivated rice and barley (*Hordeum vulgare*). Narhan[60] comprises four ceramic industries: Black and Red Ware with painting in white, black slipped ware, bed slipped ware and bed ware. A good quantity of archaeological material obtained by flotation from the middle deposits of this culture give an idea of agricultural practices. Cereal grains of hulled and six row barley, club wheat, bread wheat, dwarf and cultivated rice have been identified. The analysis of cereal grain from the black and red ware deposits from Narhan indicates that they were an intelligent lot of farmers. They also grew two cereal crops in a year, rice in summer and wheat and barley in winter. Wheat grains obtained from Pd I at Narhan belong to *Triticum sphaerococcum perc., Triticum aestivum* (L.) and *Triticum compactum.* The grains of wheat turned to be a mixture of three types and size. In a lot of 23 grains, 15 are short, broad and more or less oval in shape. Most of the grains have evenly rounded dorsal side. However a few exhibit a hump like circular area raised on their dorsal side. The grains measure 4.00-510 mm in length, 2-80-3.50 mm in breadth and 2-00-3.50 mm in thickness. Checks to the ventral furrow are rounded.Remaining 8 caryopses are somewhat elongated. Out of these 6 grains are narrower towards both the ends and slightly broader in the middle. The dorsal side is smooth and slightly raised. These caryopses measure 5.00-6.00 mm in length, 2.20-3.50mm in breadth and 2.10-2.20 mm in thickness. Rest 2 grains measure about 5-90 mm in length, 3.60 mm in breadth and 3.00 -3.10 mm in thickness. They are more or less similar in shape but differ in having one end narrower and the other broader and rounded. Further, dorsal side in these two grains is somewhat flattened and evenly rounded.

The short, broad and more or less rounded grains compare in all morphological characters with the caryopses of dwarf-wheat (*T. sphaerococcum perc.*). The grains narrower towards both the end; and thicker in the middle resemble bread wheat (*T. aestivum*). Two grains are distinguishable from these of bread wheat, being narrower towards the base and having a rounded opposite end, in contrast to the raised dorsal side. On comparison, these grains exhibit their close affinity with the grains of club wheat (*T. compactum Host.*).

Narhan wheat samples have been found to represent a mixture of dwarf-wheat (*T. sphaerococcum perc,*) bread wheat (*T. aestivum*) and club wheat (*T. compactum*).

Twenty four complete grains of barley recovered from this site belong to the hulled form of six row *Hordeum vulgare* variety.These are elongated caryopses. They measure 4.80-6.50 mm in length, 2.00-3.00 mm in breadth and 2.00-3.00 mm in thickness. The ventral furrow originates from the base and gradually wideness towards the upper end of the grains. The dorsal side is almost flat and the embryo rests on the beak like projections. Grains are enclosed, partially or completely, within a thick husk or hull. Being hulled, they lack in evenly rounded outline and are angular in shape because of longitudinal ridges and grooved impressed by the husk veins. These belong to hulled species. The hulled species of barley have been classified as two row and six row forms, depending on the number of fertile florets per node. All the species of barley belong to the same potentially inter-fertile population and are grouped under single species *Hordeum vulgare L. emend.* The Narhan barley has, therefore, been placed under the hulled, six row form of *Hordeum vulgare L. emend.*

The chalcolithic archaeobotanical remains of Senuwar[61] contained rice, barley (*Hordeum vulgare*) dwarf wheat (*Triticum sphaerococcum*) bread wheat (*Triticum aestivum*) along with other cereals.

SENUWAR

Cereals	**Neolithic 2200- 1950 B.C.**	**Neolithic Chalcolithic 1950-1300 B.C.**	**Chalcolithic period 1300-700/ 1600 B.C.**
Barley (*Hordeum vulgare*)	√	√	√
Dwarf wheat (*T. sphaerococcum*)	√	√	√
Bread wheat (*T. aestivum*)	×	√	√

√ Recorded in collection
× absent in collection

Excavation at Imlidih Khurd revealed that people of period II (Black and Red Ware culture) 1300-800 B.C. also cultivated[62] barley (*Hordeum vulgare L. emend Bowden*), wheat (*Hordeum vulgare L.,*) and *Triticum sphaerococcum perc.* like Narhan Black and Red ware phase, both in the same region of Gorakhpur district, seem to have shared much the same kind of crop economy and enjoyed mutual contacts. The plant economy of Imlidih Khurd demonstrated that approximately in the mid-second millennium B.C. wheat and barley cultivation became a firmly established economy in the Middle Gaṅgā Plain.

Period II of Narhan (Black slipped ware phase, 800-600 B.C.) includes the remains of wheat (club-*Triticum compactum,* bread-*Triticum aestivum,* dwarf- *Triticum sphaerococcum*) and barley (*Hulled* and six *row-Hordeum vulgare*).

Painted Grey Ware Culture :

The evidence of subsistence pattern of PGW people comes mainly from two sites i.e. Hastinapur and Atranjikhera. The settlers of P.G.W. culture cultivated rice, wheat, barley, pea and some other cereals. The most important cereal that was added to the diet-during the P.G.W. was wheat as it has not been found in any of the earlier culture in the Doab. On the basis of the cereal remains from Atranjikhera, it has been proved that all the three important cereals namely rice, wheat and barley were now cultivated and was used for food. The crops were grown along with the banks of the Kalinadi in the fertile alluvium annually deposited by this river. As wheat requires more water at regular intervals than barley. R.C. Gaur doubts that the P.G.W. folk were able to supply water for field irrigtion although at present there is no evidence from P.G.W. levels that some sort of irrigation was practiced. He observed that a few deep circular pits noticed outside the habitation area were infact used as *Kachcha* wells. This practice of constructing *kachcha* wells to irrigate the fields is still prevalent in the vicinity of the site. At Radhan in Kanpur, the plant economy of the overlap phase between the PGW and NBP cultures comprises of rice, barley (*Hordeum vulgare Linn.*) and common pea (*Pisum arvense*).

Early Historical :

Period III of Narhan belongs to NBPW (circa 600-200 B.C.) comprise the remains of *Oryza sativa, Hordeum vulgare* and *Triticum* etc. At Narhan a lot of 14 complete grains of hulled, six rowed form of barley from this phase, has brought into light the continued cultivation of this crop from period I. The grains measure 4.50- 7.00mm in length, 2.50-4.00mm in breadth and 2.00 -2.50 mm in thickness. While wheat are hexaploid, the caryopses 6.00-6.25 mm in length, 3.00-3.50 mm in breadth and about 2.50mm in thickness, appear elongated, slightly narrower towards, both the ends and broader in the middle and compare in all the features with bread wheat comprise the short, broad and more or less rounded to oval caryopses, which are comparable to *Triticum sphaerococcum perc.* the Indian dwarf wheat. These grains measure 41.00-5.75 mm in length, 3.50-4.00mm in breadth and 2.75-3.30mm in thickness.

All these forms of hexaploid wheat viz. *Triticum aestivum* (bread wheat). *T. compactum* (club wheat) and *T. sphaerococcum perc.*(dwarf wheat) have been encountered in Pd I. However no wheat grains could be found in Pd II. In the deposits of Pd III bread wheat and dwarf wheat have been recovered, suggesting the continuation of wheat cultivation at Narhan since 1000 B.C.

References

1. i, 23, 15; 66, 3; 117, 21; 135, 8; 176, 2; ii 5, 6; 14, ii; v. 85. 3; viii. 3, 4; viii, 2, 3; 22, 6; 63, 9; 78, 10 etc.
2. ii, 8, 3; vi, 30, I; 50, I.2; 91, I; 141, 2; 142 I.2; viii. 7, 20; ix. I 22; 6, 14; xiii, I. 42;

   Taittiriya saṁhitā, vi, 2, 10, 3; 4.10, 5; vii, 2, 10, 2; *Kathaka saṁhitā,* xxv.10; xxvi, 5; *Maitrayani Saṁhitā,* IV, 3, 2; *Vajasaneyi Saṁhitā,* v. 26; XVII, 12; xxiii, 30. *Śatapatha Brāhmaṇa,*I. I, 4; 20 iii, 5, 2 I; iii, 910
3. *Kausitaki Brāhmaṇa* IV, 13
4. *Taittiriya Saṁhitā,* viii, 2, 10.2
5. Hopkins, *Journal of the American Oriental Society,* 17, 86, 4.
6. Sowing (Vap) grain is referred to in Rv i.117, 21; ripening of grain in 135, 8; plauging (krs) in i. 176, 2. grain rejoice in rain is alluded to in ii. 5-6.
7. *Maitrayani Saṁhitā* i, 28;

   *Vaijasaneyi Saṁhitā,*xviii, 12; XIX, 22 89; xxi, 29 etc.
8. *Śatapatha Brāhmaṇa,* xii, 7. I 2; 2, 9; *Brhadaranyaka Upnishad,* vi, 3, 22 (*Madhyamdina* vi, 3, 13 *Kanva*) etc.
9. *Taittirya Brāhmaṇa,* i, 3, 7, 2
10. *Satpatha Brāhmaṇa,* xii, 9, I. 5,
11. V. 2, I.6
12. Mellart, James 1975. *The Neolithic of the Near East;* London, p. 72
13. Jarrige, J.F. and M. Lechevallier, 1977. *Excavation at Mehargarh, Baluchistan, South Asian Archaeology,* Naples, pp. 463-535.
14. Jarrige J.F. 1983. *Continuity and Change in the North Plain (Baluchistan, Pakistan) at the Beginning of the Second Millennium* B.C. MSS.
15. Constantini, L. Biasini L.C. 1985. *Agriculture in Baluchistan between the 7th and the 3rd millennium B.C. Newsletter of Baluchistan studies* 2; pp. 16-30.
16. Mittre, Vishnu 1977. *Changing Economy in India. Origins of Agriculture* (ed.) Charles A. Recd., The Hague, Paris, p. 574.
17. Kajale, M.D. 1982. Early Agriculture in the Kashmir valley, Palaeobotanical evidence from recent excavations at Gufkral, Paper read in Ahmedabad Conference in Oct. 1982.
18. Sharma, G.R. & Mandal D., 1980, *Excavation at Mahagar,* Allahabad, p. 47.
19. *IAR* 1980-81, p. 110

20. Mittre, Vishnu; Changing economy in Ancient India. *Origin of Agriculture* (ed. C. reed), Chicago: 569-88.

Mittre, Vishnu and Savithri, R. 1982, 'Food economy of the Harappan' *Harappan Civilization* (ed. G.L. Posschl). Delhi pp. 205-29.

21. Mittre, Vishnu (1972). Neolithic Plant Economy at Chirand, Bihar, *The Palaeobotanist* Vol. 21, pp. 19-21.

22. Sharma, G.R. & Mandal, D. 1980. *Excavation of Mahagara,* Allahabad, pp. 46-50.

23. Saraswat, K.S. Early farming communities of the Kaimur, *Puratattva* No. 19, 1988-89, p. 502.

24. Saraswat K.S. Seed & Fruit Remains at ancient Imlidih Khurd, Gorakhpur : A Preliminary Report, *Pragdhara,* No. 3

25. Jarrige, J.F. 1981. Economy and society in the early chalcolithic bronze age of Baluchistan, *South Asian Archaeology* 1977, (ed.) Herbert Hartel, p. 110.

26. Jarrige J.F. 1982. Excavation at Mehrgarh. *Harappan Civilization,* (ed.) Gregory L. Possehl, Delhi, pp. 79-84.

27. Constantini, L. 1984. The Beginning Of The Agriculture In The Kachi Plain: The evidence Of Mehrgarh, *South Asian Archaeology* 1981, (ed). B. Allchin, Cambridge University Press, pp. 114-115.

28. Thomas, K.D. 1981. Palaeoecological Studies In The Bannu Basin: The Sources Of Evidence, *South Asian Archaeology* 1979, (ed. H. Hartel) Berlin: pp 32-227

29. Constantini L. and Biasini, L.C. 1985 *op. cit.*

30. Saraswat, K.S. 1988 Pre and Post Harappan Crop Economy Of Ancient Rohira, Punjab, *Studies in Indian History and Culture,* (ed.) K.S. Ramchandran, Indian History And Culture Society, New Delhi, p. 229

31. Vats, M.S. 1940. *Excavation At Harappa,* Delhi, p. 466.

32. Marshall, Sir John 1931. *Mohenjodaro and Indus Civilization,* London, p. 586

33. Ibid.

34. Mittre, Vishnu and Savithri, R. *Op. cit.,* p. 208.

35. LAI, B.B., 1979, Kalibangan and the Indus Civilization, *Essays in Indian Protohistory* (eds.) D.P. Agrawal and Dilip K. Chakrabarty, Delhi, pp. 65-97.

36. Mittre, Vishnu & Savithri, R. 1982. op. cit., pp. 205-221.

37. IAR 1982-83, p. 149

38. Dikshit, K.N. 1984. The Harappan Levels at Hulas, *Man and Environment,* Vol. VIII, p. 102

39. *IAR 1983-84,* p. 177

40. *IAR 1980-81* p. 108; *IAR 1982-83*, p. 148

41. Davalikar, M.K. 1985. Early Settlement And Subsistence Patterns In The Deccan, *Recent Advances in Indo-Pacific Pre History,* (eds.) V.N. Mishra and Peter Bell Wood, New Delhi, p. 388.

42. Dhavalikar, M.K. 1984. Towards An Ecological Model for Chalcolithic Cultures Of Central and Western India, *Journal of Anthropological Archacology.* No. 3, p. 187

43. Kosambi, D.D. 1963. The Beginning Of Iron Age In India, *Journal of the Economic And Social History Of The Orient Vol.,* pp. 309-310.

44. Dhavalikar, M.K. 1988. *Excavation : The Scientific Method And The Scientific Aids, Paper Presented at the International Seminar on New Archaeology* I.C.H.R., New Delhi, 14-16 Dec. 1988

45. Dhavalikar, M.K. 1985. op. cit. p. 281-290

46. Mittre Vishnu and Savithri R. 1975-76. *Ancient Plant Economy of Inamgaon, Puratattva,* No. 8, pp. 53-62.

47. Dhavalikar, M.K. 1975-76. *Settlement Archaeology of Inamgaon, Puratattva,* No. 8, p. 47

48. Dhavalikar, M.K. 1979. *Op cit.,* p. 254.

49. Kajale, M.D. 1977. Plant Economy at Inamgaon, *Man and Environment,* Vol. I, pp. 54-56.

50. Dhavalikar, *op. cit.,* 1984, p. 145.

51. Kajale, M.D. 1977. On The Botanical findings from Excavations Of Diamabad, *Current Science,* Vol. 46 (No. 23), pp. 818-819.

52. *IAR 1980-81,* p. 108.

53. *IAR 1979-80,* p. 113.

54. Kajale, M.D. 1978. Bio Archaeology Of The Ghod Valley-Maharastra, Ph.D. Thesis, University of Pune.

55. IAR 1972-73, p. 60.

56. Chowdhary, K.A.; Saraswat, K.S. and Buth, G.M. 1977, *Ancient Agriculture and Forestry in North India,* Bombay Asia Publishing Home, p. 62.

57. Chowdhary, K.A. 1971; Plant Remains from Atranjikhera Phase III (1200-600 B.C.), *The Palaeobotanist* -20(3), pp. 280-287.

58. Saraswat, K.S. 1986. Ancient Crops Plant Remains from Sringaverpua, Allahabad (c. 1050-100 B.C.), *Geophytology* 16(1), p. 103.

59. Saraswat, K.S. 1972. The Anatomy of Living and Ancient Seed Plants-Plants Remains from Atranjikhera (c. 2000 B.C.-200 B.C.), Ph.D. Thesis A.M.U. Aligarh.

60. K.S. Saraswat, N.K. Sharma & D.C. Sahni. Plant Economy at Ancient Narhan (c. 21300 B.C.-300/400 A.D.) *Excavation at Narhan* (1984-89), pp. 255-345.

61. Saraswat K.S. *Early farming communities of the Katmur,* 1988-89, *Puratattva* No. 19, p. 502.

62. Singh, P. Imlidih-khurd, *Pragdhara* 3, 1992; *Puratattva* No. 20, 1989-90.

4

Newly Discovered Painted Rock-Shelters at Vaghai Hill

*—Kanti Kumar A. Pawar**

Rock paintings in India were first recorded by the pioneering discoveries made in 1867 by Archibald Carlyle in Mirzapur district, Uttar Pradesh. The first rock engravings of South India were brought to light by F. Fawcett in Kupgallu in 1892. Later on various scholars tried to study painted rock-shelters in a systematic way.

More than 2000 painted rock-shelters have been reported from the Indian Subcontinent grouped into central Vindhyan region, Chhota Nagpur plateau, southern Deccan region but surprisingly not a single painted rock-shelter was reported and recorded from Maharashtra. Though V.S. Wakankar had mentioned about the rock shelter in Vidarbha region of Maharastra, he did not speak on the rock-shelter paintings. Outside Maharashtra there are many painted rock-shelters i.e. in the area of Nimar, Chhindawara in M.P. north of the Vidarbha region, in the east Gupansar area in Chhattisgarh, Betamchela, Adoni, Balchaker, Hassan Patri area in Andhra Pradesh.

For the first time in Maharashtra, painted rock-shelters have been noticed at Vaghai hill (20°35'M 79° 33'E) in Chimur tahsil of Chandrapur District.

This hill locally known as "Sitamai dongar" is a part of Perjagarh range of Hills (height 431m from MSL with up throw of 131M).

On national highway leading from Nagpur to Chandrapur there is a small village Kampa about 88 km from Nagpur. On Kampa-Chimur road near about 8 kms towards west of Kampa there is another village Shankarpur. 6 kms towards south of Shankarpur village Dongargaon is located. After walking 3 kms in southern direction from

* Trainee, PGDA, ASI, Institute of Archaeology, Delhi.

Dongargaon through dense bushy forest the rock-shelters can be noticed at the top of the Vaghai hill.

Vaghai hill painted rock-shelters are divided into two parts (1) Nagargota (2) Pandubara. Nagargota rock shelter is situated in Vaghai hill, 1.2 Kms east of village Dongargaon and Pandubara is 3 Kms towards south of the same village. (Degree Sheet No. 55 p. Toposheet No. 55 P/10 of survey of India in 2 A).

Latitude - 20^0 35' 30" N. Logitude - 79^0 33' 30" E.

Altitude - 431 MSL with up throw of 141 mts. (Vaghai hill). Nagargota is about 135 M & Pandubara is about 131 M in height from the bottom of Vaghai hill.

Vaghai hill is composed of principally hillocks of rudaceous, ferruginous sand stones. Mineralogically these sandstones are composed mainly of quartz and some mica flakes. Stratigraphically this sandstone arises from 'Kamphti' formation of Mahadeo group of upper Permian to lower Triassic i.e. 280-180 million yrs B.P.

In the entire Perjagarh range and nearby dense bushy forest having vivid flora and fauna. Sag, Palash, Shisus, Babul, Mahua plants occur with various bushes, shrubs and grasses.

Deer, chital, hare, bison, panther and tiger frequently were reported earlier but nowadays with increasing human activities and continuous deforestation they are rarely found in this region.

Gond, Gowari and Mana tribes are predominant in this area. Nowadays these tribes are engaged in farming and field labour. Despite farming and labour work the Gonds have still continued their primitive work like food gathering and hunting of small animals in nearby forest. Gowaries still keep in touch with cattle grazing. Most of the Mana people are engaged in cultivation of rice.

Structure and Position of Painted Rock-Shelters at Nagargota:

On Vaghai hill a total number of 8 rock-shelters exist of which 4 rock-shelters are at Nagargota and 4 at Pandubara. The 4 rock-shelters of Nagargota run from south-west to north-east.

On the top of 4 shelters there is a huge terrace at the height of about 15 m. measuring 50 $\times$10 m. The roof of this terrace collapsed. North, south and west sides are open. The height of eastern wall is 20 m and forms a cliff and provides space for paintings. The cliff panel has a height of about 7 m. Beneath this panel 1 small cell has been observed which is man made (measuring 1.65m $\times$1.65 $\times$1.65m), having the architectural features indicating historical period. The rock shelters of Nagargota are situated on the watershed lines. The line of water divide is about 1.2 kms towards west.

The rock-shelters at Nagargota reveal paintings on roof, exterior side and cliff side. The total number of paintings are 35 among which the animal figures are 22 in number. The human figures are 13 mostly in dark red and purple red colour. The paintings typically depict *barasingha* and deer. Human figures are shown carrying metal weapons. Most of the animal paintings depict cattle and grazing animals.

The rock paintings can be categorized into two sequences.The earliest paintings are executed in dark red colour and are relatively larger. In the second stage the paintings were executed in bright red colour showing the human figures, grazing animals and horse. Animal figures have maximum height 30 cm and length 40 cm and minimum height 7 cm and length 4 cm. Some animal figures are very small in size. Out of 13, seven human figures depicted in the rock-shelters are tiny in size. 4 human figures show average size of 18 cm in height. The human figures are in dark red black colour.

Structure and Position of Painted Rock-Shelters at Pandubara:

From Nagargota these shelters are located near about 1.5 km towards east at the top of hill. There are also 4 rock-shelters at Pandubara out of which I &IV are painted.

Rock-shelter no. I faces towards North-West and 8-10 mts. below rock-shelters no. II, III, IV. Its North-South length is 44 ft.

Rock-shelters no. II, III, IV are above rock-shelter no. I Rock-shelter no. II is covered with 3 man made stone slabs and no III is covered with 4 huge dressed stone slabs.

East-west length of rock-shelter no. IV is 18 mt. North-east and west sides are open. South cliff side wall reveals more than 15 paintings. Some paintings were drawn on the ceiling.

There are 17 paintings in rock-shelters no. I and IV. Most of the paintings are drawn on bare, uneven, rough surface of cliff side wall. Out of these only 2 are human, remaining all others are of animals like deer, *barasingha*, wild boar, rhino etc. One *swastika* depiction is also there. Most of the paintings are executed in dark red, reddish brown and dark brown colour. 2 paintings are in red colour with outlining of yellow ochre colour. Size of these art forms varies in height 7 × 28 cm to 30 ×28 cms. Most of the paintings are represented individually or in groups without overlapping as compared to Nagargota. Simple human figures are painted fully and without any

Appendix-A

(Map)

MAHARASHTRA

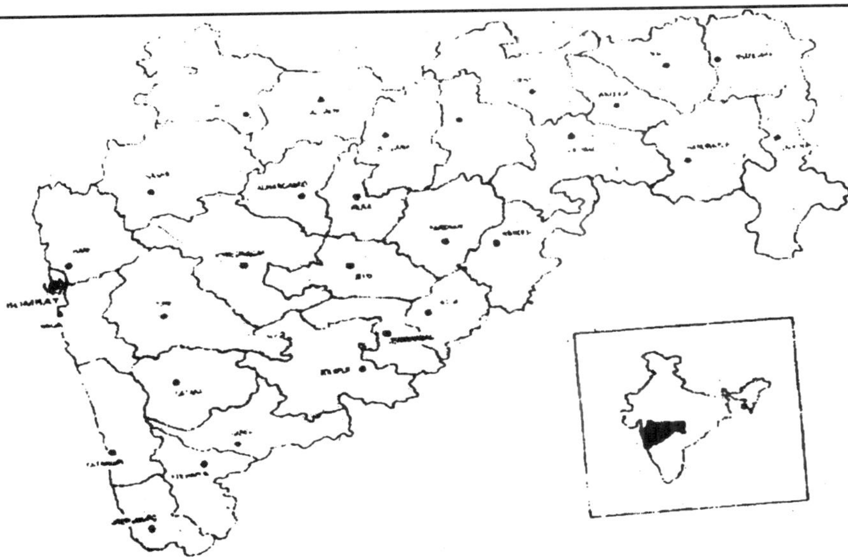

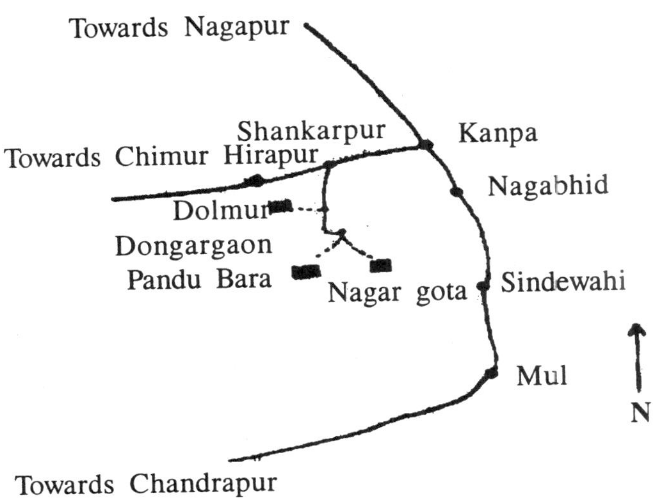

Pandu Bara painted rock shelter, 3 kms towards south of village Dongar gaon.
Post-Doms
Tq.-Chimur,
Dist.-Chandrapur. (M.S.)

Degree sheet No. 55
Topo Sheet No. 55P/10
20^0 34' 30" N. Latitude
79^0 32' 32" E. Longitute

Unproporationate Road Map

Fig 3. Vaghai : Location map.

implements arms. Outlines or body contour of animals are generally natural and fully painted. Some art forms are line drawings decorated with geometric designs.

These paintings are stereotyped, less dynamic, static, simplified and naturalistic. Some paintings show running, walking, grazing postures. All these paintings are stylistic and thematic.

Chronology:

The most vital issue of rock paintings is chronology. The earliest paintings may represent individual figures but gradually the paintings in groups show stylistic change. The first group of paintings of Nagargota appears to be of Mesolithic period (8000-10000 years BP). The most significant evidence in the present context is, however, the recovery of mircroliths. But such type of implements are not reported at Pandubara while the paintings are comparatively similar to Nagargota paintings. The style, technique and colour depicted in the paintings are similar to Bhimbetka and Panchmarhi paintings.

These important rock-shelters and the paintings are being disturbed and destroyed by the local people.

Associated Finds:

On the floor of rock-shelter at Nagargota many non-geometric microliths were found which may belong to early Mesolithic period. On the same shelter handmade and wheel made potsherds were found and in one stone slab 11 parallel grooves were noticed. On the Vaghai hill some middle Paleolithic tools and cairn circles were observed. About 4 km away from this hill before Dongargaon, Megalithic dolmens are present in good condition.

Conclusion:

It is a very important site because material evidence shows continuous cultural occupation (Middle Paleolithic-Mesolithic-Megalithic-historical). The rock-paintings flourished in the pre-historic period and continued to develop in the historical period. The prehistoric paintings essentially display the faunal world executed by the common man as they observed them. The technique and style was both in silhouette and outline.

Acknowledgement:

Profound thanks are due to Adv. Ganesh Halkare with whose help I was able to prepare this paper. I am very thankful to Prof. D.K. Bhattacharya whose able guidance and moral support gave me spirit to write this paper.

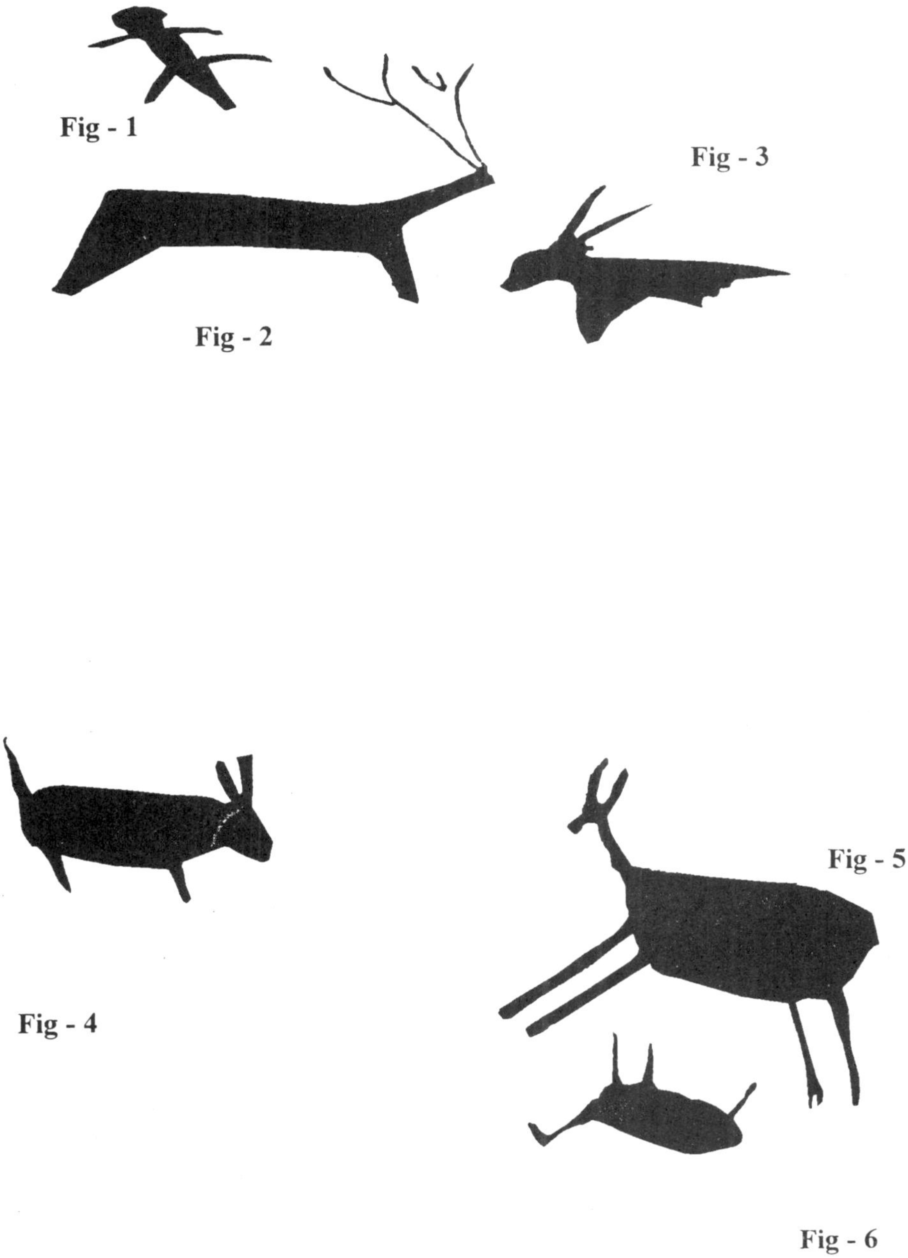

Fig. 4- Vaghai: Rock Paintings

Fig-8

Fig-7

Fig-9

Fig-10

Fig-11

Fig-12

Fig-13

Fig. 5-Vaghai Rock Paintings

Fig-14

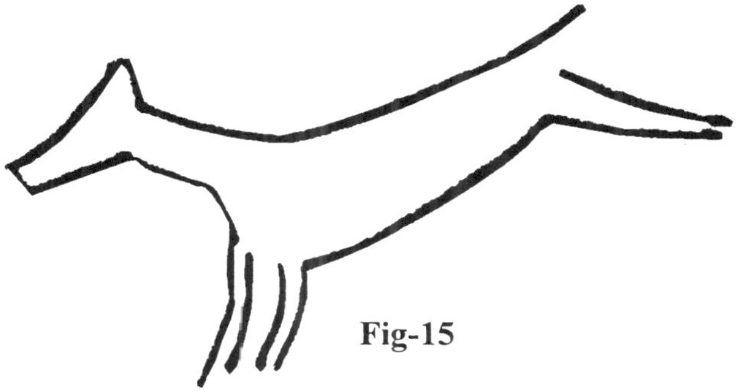

Fig-15

Fig-16

Fig-17

Fig-18

Fig-19

Fig-20

Fig. 6—Vaghai Rock Paintings

5

Water Harvesting in Harppan Culture for Various Purposes

*—Ramakant P. Dubey **

Development of culture is directly related with the development of economic condition of the society and obviously in a country like India where agriculture was, and still remains, the source of income, the availability of water plays very vital role. History testifies that human development and water have an unbreakable relationship. Today the whole world faces a grave problem of not having enough safe drinking water. The causes of this problem are increase in human population, industrialization, deforestation, air and water pollution etc. The UNO, specially UNESCO, has repeatedely warned countries about the crisis. The proportion of safe drinking water as compared to water in general is said to be as less as half a tea spoon, in half a litre of water. Thus water for human use is a major cause of concern today. This problem is even more relevant for the Indian subcontinent. India does not lack in annual rainfall but still does not have conducive geographical features to control rain water for its optimum use. In such diverse situations proper conservation and harvesting of water may prove beneficial for the country. This was understood very well by people in ancient times, and therefore many steps were taken by them to harvest and collect water.

In ancient times great civilization's like Mayan, Sumerian, Harappan etc. existed and each of these had their own typical system of controlling, conserving and harvesting water for human use.

In India during the Indus valley civilization water control, collection, and harvesting was also an important aspect of the society. They had developed several methods of storing water, protection from flood and managing excess water. Archaeological evidenses from Harappan sites also testify to their water harvesting

* Research Fellow & Part Time Lecturer V. N. G. I. A. S. S., Nagpur.

knowledge. Such sites have been found from Afghanistan in the north-west to Alamgir in U.P. and from Harappa to Bhagwatrao on the bank of 'Narmada' river.

In pre-Haprappan civilization Gabarbunds are seen in Afghanistan. In Harappan period, the Great-Bath from Mohenjodaro, Dockyard from Lothal, water plant from Dholavira and so many wells indicate the presence of water harvesting systems in this civilization. The description is as follows :

1) Gabarbunds :

Gabarbund is a type of dam which is found in Baluchistan. In Persian the meaning of the term is "dam of stones."[1] This dam was constructed perhaps for the use of drinking and irrigation. Gabarnbuds were constructed at the bottom of hilly regions by controlling rain-water. There were numerous benefits of this system like water for drinking, irrigation, fertility of soil for agriculture purposes and increasing the unerground water table. In the hilly regions of Baluchistan different techniques were used for constructing such bunds. Several examples of Gabarbunds are seen here.

Generally the Gabarbunds were made of 2 to 4 feet high platferms, placed one upon the other succesively receding in size towards the top. Each platform was made of parrallel walls of roughly dressed stoned, filled with rubble consisting of mud, stones etc. Thus they were made at the base of hills in the from of dams for conserving the flow of water from higher hilly regions. In another type of Gabarbunds the dam walls were made of stones joined together in order to make a wall. Lime and other binding materials were used. The size of the dressed stones was generally 4 ×21/2 × 1 ¼ ft^2. These dams were usually very large in size. The Gabarbund in the Bahol valley is approximately 100 feet wide. Here whatever is remaining is 80 feet long 70 feet in height. In the same context, the Gabarbund situated in Musefarilak in the Hab river valley is 100 ft. wide × 30 ft in hight. The Ahmad band in the Sarona valley is 2350 feet long and is made of dressed stones of uniform size, measuring 5' ×6.10'. The construction of these Gabarbunds show the high level of engineering and technical skill prevalent during those times. Archaeologists assign different reasons for the construction of these dams. Buhler and Lambricks assign water storage and soil conservation as the main reasons for the construction of these dams. Whereas Rikey and Disen believe that these were made not ony for collection of annual rainwater, but other resources like underground springs etc. were also used to fill up these dams.

The Great Bath of Mohenjodaro :

This may be taken as an important example of water collection and storage, Several historians have given various theories for the construction of this tank or bath, as it is popularly known. Sir John Marshall has given religious reasons for its construction like the use of water for cleaning, purification etc. He states that this bath was used for community bathing on religious occasions. The main pool was surrounded by serveral small bathrooms. A well was made near the pool to supply water for it. The pool was also provided with drains for disposing of waste water. It is on the basis that Marshall stated that the Great Bath may have been used for religious purpose[3].

Geographical conditions were favourite in Mohenjodaro for such a type of work. Due to the Indus river, the ground water level of the city was high and rainfall was good as compared to modern days. The citedal area was selected for the safety. Great Bath was constructed on the north-western area.

Technical Highlights of the Great Bath :

1) The bath is 39 ft. in the North-South direction. The width is 23 ft. and the depth is 8 ft.

2) Flights of steps have been provided in the northern and southern sides for access to the pool.Three pillars have been made on the top level of these sides.The steps are made of baked bricks.The material used for binding the bricks is said to be some material brought down from the foothills of Baluchistan, possibly bitumen ?

3) The floor of the pool has been made water proof, displaying the knowledge of civil engineering.

4) A drain was provided on the south-western corner of the pool, which was connected to a larger drain outside the complex.

5) Passages leading to small rooms, possible for ablutions and changing, were provided on three sides of the pool.

6) A well was provided as a source of water for the pool. It was situated in one of the rooms on the eastern side. A double course of baked was provided around the well for stability. However, the method of drawing water from the well could not be ascertained. Perhaps sturdy leather bags (muscak) were used for this purpose.

7) On the Northern side of the bath, two rows of eight bathrooms have been made. They are 7½ ×6 ft, in size. Great care was taken in making these bathrooms and their doors opened only on the inner side.[4]

Several sites of the Indus civilization have been discovered and excavated in recent times, but the Great Bath of Mohenjodaro is a solitary example and the technical prefection displayed in its construction is noteworthy.

The Dockyard from Lothal :

The economy of the civilization was largely dependant on commerce and trade, as evidenced from the excavated towns and cities. As most of these sites are situated on river banks and coastal areas a large part of the trading activities may have been dependant on water ways and sea routes. Several evidences of architecture specially planned for this purpose have been discovered at Harappan sites. In this context, reference may be made to the dockyard discovered from Lothal. This may be taken as an outstanding example of water control and harvesting for trade purposes. The technique of constructing this dockyard shows the great engineering skill of the Indus valley people. The Bhogawa river, which presently flows some distance away form the site, may have flowed adjacent to the ancient Lothal city. A long channel from this river was constructed to divert the water to the dockyard to maintain its water level at all times. Thus, ships could dock at Lothal, irrespective of high or low tide. In this way, Lothal may have been an important port city for overseas trade.

The Technical Features of the Dockyard :

The dockyard is rectangular in shape, 219 m in the North-South and 38 m in the East-West direction. Baked bricks were used for construction. According to archaeologists the depth of dockyard was 4.15 m. The inner walls of the dockyard were made exactly perpendicular to the floor to facilitate loading and unloading of ships. The northern side of the dockyard was provided with a 12 m wide door for entering ships and a sluice gate, probably provided with a wooden plank, was made on the southern side for the discharge of excess water. However, care was taken to maintain the water level in the dockyard for the easy entry and exit of ships. Archaeologists are of the opinion that ships as large as 18 to 20 feet and weighing 60 to 75 tons could be accommodated in this dockyard. The excess water discharged from the dockyard may have been used for irrigation purposes. Thus, the geographical features of this area were used to the maximum advantage by the people of the area.

Water-Harvesting and Storage at Dholavira :

The ancient site of Dholavira is situated in Kutch in Western Gujarat. The climatic conditions of this area may have been similar to present times with minor variations. The site of Dholavira is situated on the Rann of Kutch which was surrounded by saline water of the Arabian sea. Therefore water for domestic use may have been a scarcity.

Manhar on the south and Mansar on the North-East are the nullahs carrying rain-water that appear to have flowed close to this ancient city. These channels were watered only during the monsoon season, therefore dams were constructed on them to control the run-off. Two dams were constructed on the Manhar channel to control

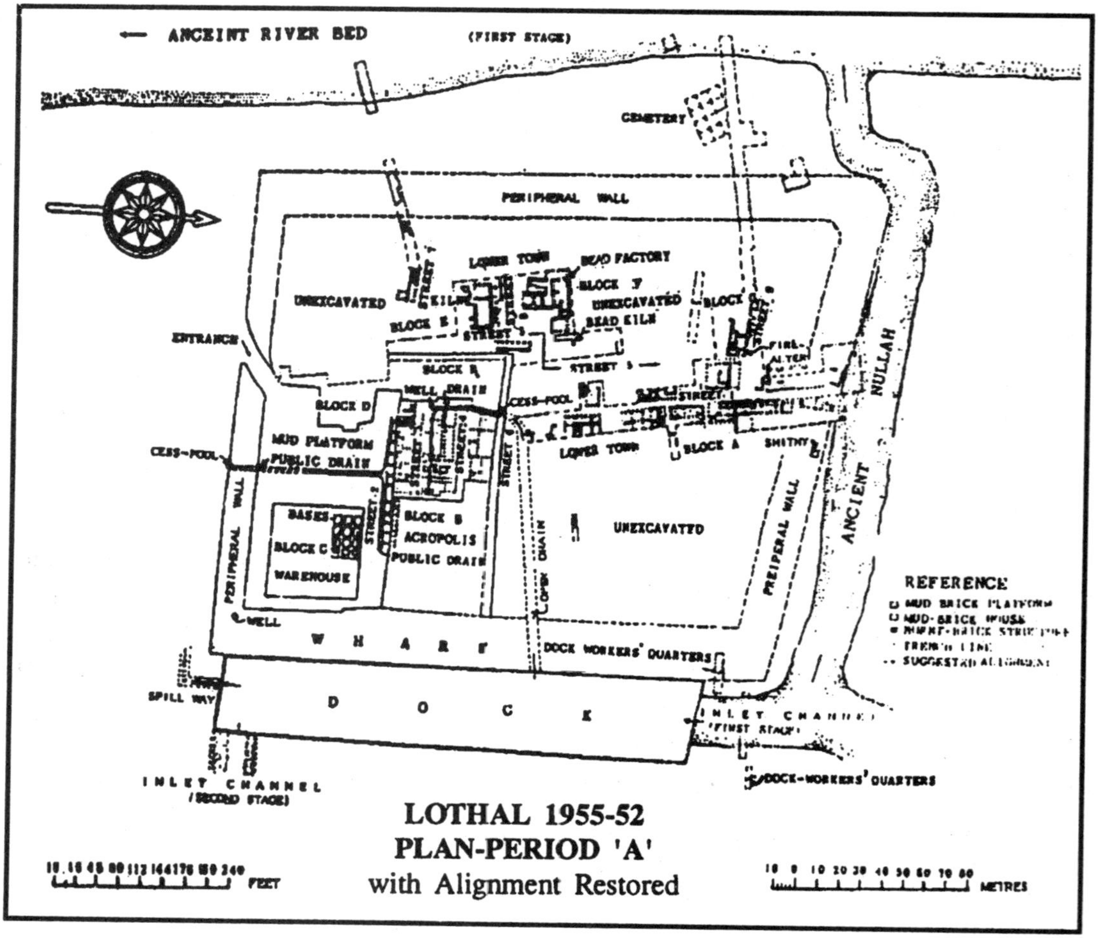

Fig. 7-Dubey, Lothal : Plan Period 'A'

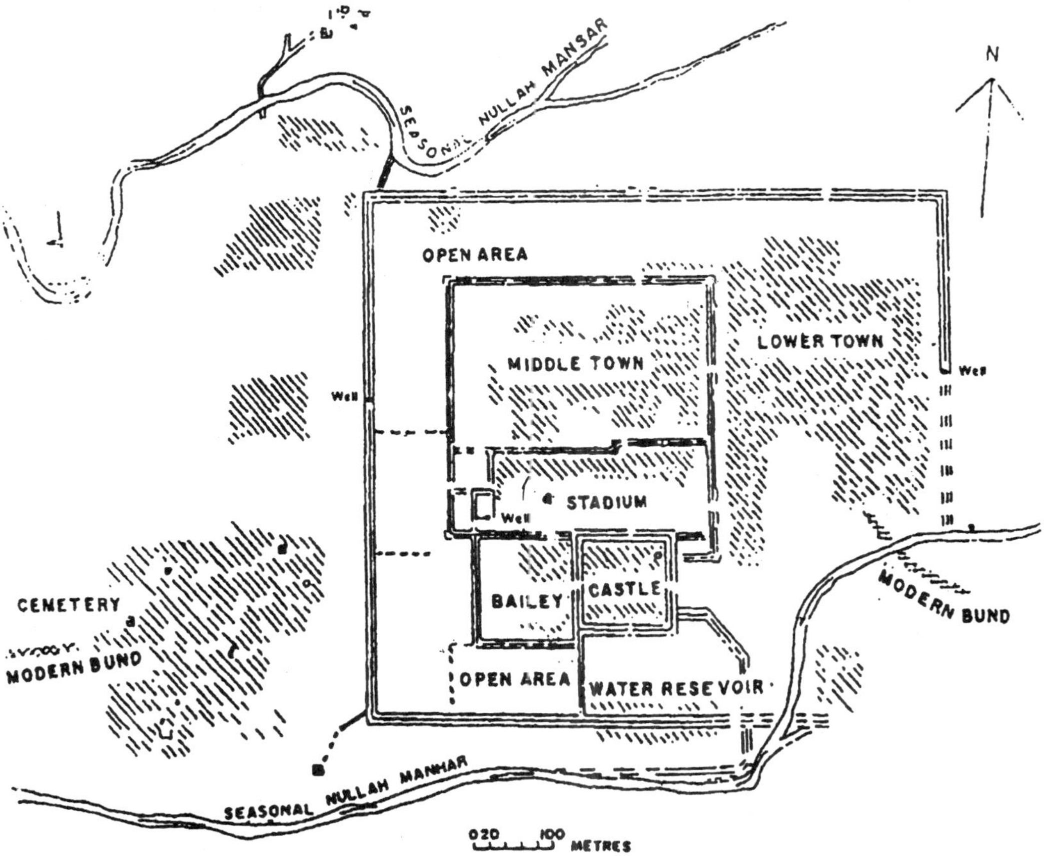

Fig. 8-Dubey Dholavira: Layout of Harappan Settlement

the flow of water, as revealed by excavations. This water was directed to a nearby tank measuring 7 sq.m. through a channel, within the fortified city of Dholavira.A small drain some feet above the floor level, has been provided in the south-western corner of the tank to drain out excess water. The main purpose of this type of water harvesting at Dholavira may have been to collect water for domestic use.

Another example of water harvesting has also been discovered from this site. During excavations a well measuring 4 m in diameter was found, which was lined with dressed stones. A vertical slab measuring 1.33 m ×1.43 m was put vertically on the broader side of the horizontal covering slabs. On the south western corner of the vertical slab a semicircular hole was made through which water from the well was discharged to a tank, through a stone-lined channel for water collection.

This drain or channel was also covered with stone slabs. The tank, made for collecting water form the well, was 4.35 m long in the north-south direction, 2.95 m, broad and 3.58 m deep. The base of the tank was lined with rectangular stone slabs and the walls were made of stone rubble masonry. Another smaller tank, measuring 78 ×6 ×5 cm. was made at the base of this larger tank. This small tank was provided with steps. The rope marks for drawing water have also been discovered on the slabs used in the well. Probably tough leather bags were used to draw water from wells.

Wells from Indus Valley Civilization :

Numerous wells have been discovered from the sites of the Indus valley civilization. About 600 wells have been discovered from the city of Mohenjodaro itself[5].

1) All the wells are circular.
2) Most of the wells are brick-lined, however some wells made of stone have also been found.
3) They measure from 2 feet to 4 feet in diameter.
4) Wedge-shaped bricks have been used to contruct these wells.
5) A variety of brick shapes may be seen in the various wells.
6) Two types of wells have been found from the Indus civilization sites (a) Private (b) Public.
7) They are maximum 50 feet in depth.
8) Provision was made to keep earthen pots for filling water.
9) The wells were also provided with drains to discharge dirty water.

Thus, the various modes of constructions and planning of structures for conserving, storing and harvesting water may be seen in the Harappan sites. The

Gabarbunds were made to collect water for irrigation and domestic use. The Great Bath from Mohenjodaro may have been made for religious purposes. The Dockyard at Lothal was made for trade purposes. In the same way structures like tanks, wells and channels ware made at Dholavira for the use of sub-terranean water. It is evident from all the above-mentioned examples that the people of the Indus Valley Civilization understood the importance of water and deviced several ways to conserve it. In fact, our modern water-harvesting system may also take inspiration from these ancient, traditional systems.

References

1. Shendge Malti J., *The Civilised Demons : The Harappans in Ṛg Veda,* New Delhi 1977, p. 233.
2. Ibid.
3. Marshall John, *Mohenjo-Daro & The Indus Valley Civilization,* Vol. III, London 1931, p. 145.
4. Wheeler, Sir Mortimer, *Indus Civilization* (II Edi.), London 1962, p. 31.
5. Rao S. R., *Dawn and Devolution of the Indus Civilization,* New Delhi 1991, p. 56.

6

Beads from Mahisdal

—*Mohan Chandra Joshi**

Human kind has always an aesthetic sense and creativity. From time immemorial he has invented many things to make him beautiful and charming. Mankind has an inherent virtue to adorn himself. Beads are such decorative things, which had been practiced since ancient times. Beads are perforated objects, which are strung and used as ornaments. The earliest records of beads in India are found from the upper Palaeolithic and Mesolithic times but bead-making as an industry developed fully from Proto-historic period onwards. Beads are important part of socio-economic pattern of different times. The most common medium used for making beads are terracotta, semi-precious stones, shell, bone, glass, and lac, etc. Metals like gold, silver, copper have also been used but rarely.

The present work highlights a broad outline on beads revealed from Mahisdal excavation with an intention to provide some informative data, which may unfold a few unknown facts. The present study has been made with the help of data available so far.

Before the discussion on beads, a brief account about the site of Mahisdal seems to be essential. The site known as Mahisdal (23°-43' N and 87°-42' E) is located on the bank of the river Kopai below the northern end of the railway bridge over the Kopai near Santiniketan in district Birbhum, West Bengal. Shri R.P. Das of the Eastern Circle (presently known as Kolkata Circle) of the Archaeological Survey of India undertook the small scale excavation in the year 1963-64. The main objective of the excavation was to ascertain the Chalcolithic culture in West Bengal. The site measuring 230 meters long and 135 meters wide rising some five meters above the surrounding ground level had a cultural deposit of only 2-meters at its maximum. Excavation revealed

---

*Assistant Archaeologist, ASI, Lucknow Circle.

two cultural periods without any break; the later characterized by the use of iron. The C14 dates put the beginning of period I at Mahisdal around the middle of the second millennium B.C.[1]

In case of Mahisdal, I.A.R., 1963-64 gives very little information on beads. The full report on antiquities recovered from the site is still awaited. Perhaps the provided data could help in comparative study of beads found from other excavated sites of West Bengal as well as beads discovered from the rest of India.

Thirty-nine beads were recovered from Mahisdal. The medium used in making beads are terracotta, glass, shell, steatite and semi-precious stones i.e. agate, carnelian, and chert. Amongst all, agate beads are found largest in number. Though the detail, in respect of distribution of beads with periodization is not available, yet the following chart can provide their stratigraphical context:

S.No.	**Material**	**Layers**										
		1	1A	1B	2	2A	2B	3	4	5	6	**Total**
1.	Agate	-	-	5	10	-	-	1	1	1	1	19
2.	Glass	-	-	-	2	1	-	1	-	-	-	4
3.	Shell	-	-	-	3	1	-	-	-	-	-	4
4.	Carnelian	-	-	1	-	-	-	1	1	-	-	3
5.	Steatite	-	-	-	-	-	-	-	1	-	2	3
6.	Terracotta	-	-	-	2	-	-	-	-	-	-	2
7.	Red Chert	-	-	-	1	-	-	-	-	1	-	2
8.	Qartz	-	-	-	-	-	-	-	-	1	-	1
9.	Aquamarine	-	-	-	-	-	-	-	-	1	-	1
												39

(A) Beads of Agate

Out of 19 agate beads, majority are made of banded variety unlike two beads which are having one single black colour. These beads are distributed in layers 1b, 2, 3, 4, 5, and 6. Ten beads were encountered from stratum 2. The lengths of these beads vary from 0.4 cm. to 1.6 cm. Unusually one bead which is half broken probably had length of 3.2 cm. Diameters range from 0.4cm. to 1.7 cm. So far as typology is concerned, these are short cylinder circular, short barrel circular, long barrel circular, truncated short cylinder, oval, biconvex circular and short biconvex in shape. Agate beads have various kinds of coloured bands including black and white, light orange and white, white and light grey, light brown and white, smokey grey and white, black and smokey grey. Few of them are remarkable for their workmanship. The following specimens (Pl. I A, 1-12) are illustrated below:

1. Biconvex circular, half broken; bearing black and white bands where white bands only on the edge; L. 0.5 cm. B. 1.5 cm.
2. Biconvex circular with white and light grey bands; L. 0.6 cm. B. 1.4 cm.
3. Variant of no. 2. One side of the bead is having smokey white colour whereas alternate bands of white, black and smokey white colour are seen on the other side of the bead. L. 0.6; B. 1.4 cm.
4. Variant of no. 2 and 3. The colour of the bands are white and light brown. L. 0.6 cm. B. 1.4 cm.
5. Short cylinder circular having black and smokey grey bands. L. 0.5 cm. B. 0.8 cm.
6. Variant of no. 2. L. 0.5 cm. B. 1.3 cm.
7. Truncated short cylinder oval with light brown and grey coloured bands. L. 0.4 cm. B. 0.6 cm.
8. Bi-conical hexagon with black and white bands. L. 1.6 cm. B. 0.4 cm.
9. Same as no 8 with light orange and white bands. L. 1.3 cm. B. 0.6 cm.
10. Short barrel circular with orange and white bands. L. 0.8 cm. B. 1.0 cm.
11. Long barrel circular with tri-coloured bands of white, orange and reddish brown. L. 1.5 cm. B. 0.4 cm.
12. Half-broken, long barrel circular with orange and white bands. L. 1.6 cm. B. 0.7 cm.

(B) Beads of Carnelian:

Only three specimens were found. Interestingly, one bead is of *etched* variety, one bead is tiny conical and second one is micro-circular bead. Besides, etched bead is of biconical variety. Conical bead is very unusual and found very rare in chalcolithic context in West Bengal. The length of these beads vary from .2 cm. to 1.3 cm. and breadth range from 0.1 cm. to 0.6 cm. All three beads have been reported from strata Ib, 3 and 4 respectively. The brief description (Pl. I-B1-3) of these beads is as under.

1. Micro circular bead; L. 0.1 cm. B.0.2 cm.
2. A tiny conical bead; L. 0.7 cm. B. 0.5 cm.
3. Etched bi-conical bead. Etching is achieved by zonal bands. However some of the bands have become blurred L. 1.3 cm. B. 0.6 cm.

(C) Beads of Glass:

Five glass beads, all opaque, were recovered from the excavation at Mahisdal in three colours i.e. sky blue, orange and black. These are distributed in layers 2, 2a and 3. The shape does not indicate much variety. The most common shape being short barrel circular, truncated short barrel. From the dimensional point of view the average length and breadth of the glass beads vary from 0.6 cm. to 0.9 cm. and 0.3 cm. to 0.8 cm. respectively. The brief description (Pl. I-B, 4-6) of glass bead is as below:

1. Truncated short barrel circular of sky blue colour. L. 0.9 cm. B. 0.8 cm.
2. Short barrel circular of orange colour. L. 0.6 cm. B. 0.5 cm.
3. Short barrel circular in black colour. L. .6 cm. B. 0.3 cm.

(D) Steatite:

All three beads are disc shaped of which two micro types are having same size measuring 0.1 cm. (length) ×0.2 cm. (breadth). One of them is given in Pl.I-B, 7. One bead is comparatively thin and half-broken. These beads are found associated with the layers 6 and 4.

(E) Beads of Terracotta:

Two beads in terracotta are noticed in the layer 2. The surface of these beads is not so smooth. Typologically, one bead is of long cylinder circular variety (Pl. I-B, 12) measuring 3.5 cm ×1.5 cm. and second one being truncated bi-conical (Pl. I-B, 13) measuring 1.2 cm ×1.2 cm.

(F) Beads of Shell:

Four tiny shell beads, all short barrel, circular types have been discovered from the excavation. One bead is half-broken. These are reported from the layer 2 and 2a. Interestingly, three beads are of same size i.e. 0.6 cm. (length) ×.3 cm. (breadth), while other one (Pl. I-B, 8) measures 0.12 cm. (length) ×0.3 cm. (breadth).

(G) Beads of Chert:

The illustrated examples (Pl. B, 9-10) are as under.

1. Short barrel circular, broken. L. .9 cm. B. 0.4 cm.
2. Disc-shaped L. 0.3 cm. B. .6 cm.

(H) Beads of Quartz:

Only one bead made of quartz which is of micro-circular type is noticed. The length of this bead is 0.1 cm. and 0.4 cm. respectively.

(I) Bead of Aquamarine:

One bead made of aquamarine is reported which is hexagonal at the corner and light green in colour. This is of etched variety (Pl. I-B, 11).

Conclusion:

So far as typology of the beads of Mahisdal is concerned these are comparable with those from Chandraketugarh (Sharmy Chakraborty. Beads from Chandraketugarh *Pratna Samikṣā*), Dumdum (Beads of Dumdum). Since no bead-manufacturing industry has been reported from the site at Mahisdal, the yields seem to be imported from outside. In the light of very limited information on beads, it is difficult to understand the complete aspect of bead making and its distribution pattern and therefore it becomes necessary to find out the main site of bead-making industry in West Bengal.

Acknowledgement:

I am grateful to Dr. B. Bandopadhyay, Superintending Archaeologist, Kolkata Circle, Archaeological Survey of India who allowed me to deal with the material of Mahisdal. I am also thankful to Shri Indu Prakash, Assistant Superintending Archaelogist, Lucknow Circle, Archaeological Survey of India for providing valuable suggestions.

References

1. *Indian Archaeology* 1963-64, A Review.
2. Chakraborty, Sharmy. Beads from Chandraketugarh, *Pratna Samikṣā*, D.A., M.W.B., Vol. III & IV.
3. Joshi, Mohan Chandra. Beads from Dumdum Excavation: At a Glance, *Pragdhara*, U.P.S.A.D., Lucknow (in press).

7

Daradas (Dards) : Their Folk and Tribal Art Traditions

—*Dr B.R. Mani**

The ancient tribal clans of the Daradas, generally mentioned as Dards or Monpas and Drokpas, distinct among the people in Ladakh who mostly adopted Tibetan form of Buddhism after the ninth century onwards, remained powerful and politically very strong in the regions north of Kashmir, spread from the Hindukush mountains in the west to Tibetan borderlands in the east around the Kingdom of Na-ri during *circa* 700 to 900 A.D. Ladakh came under direct possession of Nyima-Gon who was great-grandson of Tibetan King Lang-dar-ma who was assassinated in 842 A.D. At the time of his death, Nyima-Gon had divided his Kingdom amongst his three sons who ruled in Ladakh, Guge and Purang and thereafter Ladakh was ruled by the Kings of another dynasty who traced their origin from Tibet. The Tibetan inscriptions on boulders near Saspol bridge on way to Alchi have been assigned to the period 760 to 840 A.D. on the basis of orthography and onomastics[1] and suggests the inroads of Tibetan armies during the eight and ninth centuries A.D. after which Tibetan culture engulfed the region in the following centuries.Thus it is quite evident that the period till the end of the ninth century A.D. in Ladakh had negligible influence of Tibetan Buddhism, though Buddhism had already spread in the region, mainly due to its impacts from Kashmir and Gilgit-Chitral regions as confirmed from the huge rock-cut images of Maitreya at Mulbekh, Apati and Kartse Khar and sculptures at Drass[2] which can be placed during the period of C.700 to 900 A.D. when the area was under the control of local tribal clans.

Indo-Iranian (Dardic) and Mongoloid (Tibetan) elements have been traced in the racial features of the present day Ladakhi population which is mostly following

* Director (Archaeology), Archaeological Survey of India, Janpath, New Delhi.

Buddhism in Leh district and Islam in Kargil district. Islamic conversion was mainly initiated in the fifteenth century A.D. through the influence of the Sultans of Kashmir in Ladakh and Baltistan. The entire region was known as Dardistan or the land of the Dard or Sanskrit Darada tribe, which finds mention in geographical lists of the *Purāṇas* and *Mahābhārata* as neighbours of Dārvas, Śūras, Audumbaras, Kashmīras and Trigartas[3], which has been called by the classical Greek writers[4] Strabo and Megasthenes as Derdai, Daradrai of Ptolemy and Dardae of Pliny who collected gold from the piled up heaps of earth dug in the ground in winter by the 'gold digging ants', apparently identified[5]as the large size rats still noticed making barrows in Zanskar and other regions along the Indus. That Daradas were producing and dealing in gold is further evidenced by the fact that till 1908 Kargil remained the centre of gold trade.[6] The scions of the ancient Daradas or Dards are supposed to be present day Indian Drokpas of Da Hanu area and the Monpas in Ladakh besides the inhabitants of Skardu, Gilgit and Hunza and those living along the Karakorum highway across the LOC. The Drokpas identified as Dards are famous for their sharp and beautiful features and they love flowers and beads and decorate their hairdo and caps with them. They speak Balti language and practice their own socio-religious system besides Buddhism and celebrate the festival of flowers called *Men-tok Stan-mo* on an auspicious day selected by an On-po (astrologer), as part of the big harvest festival called *Srub-lha.*[7] Similarly the *Shon-rches* dance[8], performed in circle, mostly in honour of Dorje Chenmo, is supposed to have its origin in the Gilgit area under the Monpas. Songs like *Shon-glu* and *Bal-glu* which originated in Baltistan became very common in the entire region of Baltistan and Ladakh which were sung along with the dances. During the medieval times Baltistan remained a territory under the Kingdom of Ladakh ruled by clan chiefs called Cho who had adopted Islam later and their descendents are still living in the villages in the region. The Monpas in Ladakh have mainly adopted the profession of singing and dancing and they are invited to perform their skill on festive occasions and rituals.

Thus we have three distinct phases of chronological development associated with the tribal clans of the Daradas - the earliest phase of Prehistoric times when they were hunters and gatherers, the middle phase when they adopted somewhat settled life of pastorals and nomads. With the advent of the Kushans in the region, in an era of intercontinental trade developments, helped them in exchange of commodities and started adopting more civilized ways of living than before. It was around the first century B.C. to sixth century A.D. that they became famous as Daradas (Derdai, Daradrai or Dardae) and found place in classical and other literary works as an organized tribe and became a political power till the ninth century A.D. after which in the last and the third phase they merged in the new social order created due to introduction of Tibetan Buddhism and Tibetan people settling in the region followed by Islam in the fifteenth Century A.D. in the western part of the region including Kargil area and particularly in Gilgit, Chitral and Baltistan. Giuseppe Tucci[9] on the basis of various names of Darada rulers and their attacks over the Kingdom of Kashmir as described in *Rājataranginī,* distinguishes them to be Hindus stating that perhaps Buddhism had not been altogether forgotten. I do not agree with him as I think that the names of Darada rulers such as Achalamangala in the reign of Ananta (1028-1063 A.D.), one during the time of Harsha (1089-1111 A.D.) and Darada ruler Jagaddala during the time of Uchchhala (1101-1111A.D.) and Darada ruler Maṇidhara during the time of Sussala (1112-1120 A.D.) are Indian names which can be related to both Buddhism or Hinduism. Tucci's contention that mention of Darada ruler Achalamangala alongwith seven mlechchha princes suggests that some understanding between the Daradas and Muslims had already started in the region in eleventh century, seems to be convincing. In some of the references of Daradas in connection with the conquest of Lalitāditya Muktāpīḍa, Kalhaṇa states that the king could not tolerate the strong alcohol of the Daradas[10]. Kalhaṇa calls Lalliya Shāhī ruler as sandwitched between the Darada and the Turuṣka kings.[11]

The prehistoric phase of the Daradas is represented mainly by the petroglyphs discovered in Ladakh as well as on the other side of the LOC along the Karakorum highway. So far as prehistoric remains in Ladakh are concerned, stone artifacts in the forms of unifacial breccia chopper, three bifacial quartzite hand axes and a retouched worked block of breccia belonging to the Lower Paleolithic assemblage have been found at Alchi on the left bank of the Indus by the Prehistory Branch of the Archaeological Survey of India.[12] It was noticed that the rock engravings particularly those on boulders in river valleys, mostly embedded into the ground at varied depths, are the earliest remains of the cultural heritage of Ladakh as they depict scenes of prehistoric, early historical and later historical life of man and culture in the region. The earliest ones are represented by animal figures of ibex, cattle, yak, goat, deer, dog, wolf, horse and human figures including those in hunting with bow and arrow or with spear and in dancing positions in groups, horse riders, fighting scenes and symbols of sun, palm, swastika and others. They were sometimes copied in later periods also as are evident from overlappings and scratchings without patina and looking fresh on granitic boulders. During the survey of a stretch of 25 km from Sanjak to Batalik in Balti speaking area, 2 km north-west of Sanjak at Tilichang a rock shelter was noticed with primitive engravings including several group dance scenes, men with triangular body, deer and ibexes and such scenes can also be seen on boulders 2 km ahead at Bēma and further 2 km ahead at Rugdus. Amongst prehistoric engravings noticed at Thalpan-Ziyarat datable to 3rd-2rd millennium B.C.[13] which represent the folk tradition can be mentioned boulders with hunting scene, footprint and palm print including the representation of a cult deity with crescent shaped feet, squarish face and crown with radiating lines.

The petroglyphs of the early historic phase are dominated by the representation of ibex figures and their hunting scenes. Regarding engravings of ibex figures on boulders and rocks, it is well known that it represents the local tradition of the area connected with the ceremony of ibex hunting, known as *thuma saling,* a term perhaps of Balti language, as also observed by A.H. Dani according to whom 'the story refers to a ritual conception of a male ibex, which, if drawn on this Rock, would lead to human pregnancy.[14] This is in the context of Hunza rock which is also applicable to other places of the region. The male organ of ibexes are also drawn at a number of places.

It has been the custom in Ladakh as observed by Francke during his tours[15] that on the occasion of the birth of a child, presents of 'flour-ibex' i.e. the figures of ibex made of flour and butter were offered as thanks giving and people also used to go to the pre-Buddhist places of worship in particular, to pray to be blessed with children.

Fertility cult was very popular during the early historical period in India, especially during the Kuṣāṇa period when terracotta figurines of Naigameśa and Naigameśī were modeled on large scale and offered in cult worship. They had the face of goat over human body. On the basis of the epic mythology and ancient texts like *Kalpaśūtra, Nemināthacharita* and *Antagada-Dasāɔ,* it has been suggested that the deity was worshipped to attain progeny and to take care of the evil influences occurring in the form of sickness.[16]

The ibex figures found on boulders and rocks which are also related to such ritualistic offerings may suggest their dating along with other associated engravings to the period around the beginning of the Christian era when the nomads of the region entered into social order with the impact of Kushans who besides bringing about Buddhist missionaries also encouraged trade and commerce along this region with the trading centres on the silk route.

Leh, the capital of Ladakh, seems to have developed into a city as it was the meeting place of various traders and cultural missionaries trecking along divergent trade routes coming from south of the Himālayas connecting main land of the country and also from Tibet via Kailash-Mansarovar and Nyoma on one side and extending towards north via Nubra valley to Khotan, Yarkand, Kyzil and Kashgar in the Chinese Turkistan where at Koutcha around Kyzil at the end of the seventh century A.D. there were 100 monasteries with about 5000 monks as informed by the Chinese pilgrims Huen-tsang and I-Ising and towards west via Khalatse, Batalik, Gilgit and Chitral to the area of Wakan under the Kushan empire. Such prehistoric and early historical engravings on boulders can be traced upto mountain passes of Ras-Koh towards south-west of Oxus across Indus basin in Baluchistan area.[17]

The Kushan establishments of cities founded by Hushka, Jushka and Kanishka, as mentioned in the *Rājatarangiṇī* of Kalhaṇa which can be located between Baramulla and Srinagar, were also connected with the above mentioned route via Drass and Khalatse from where ancient remains, sculptures and inscriptions have been found. The so called Kanika chorten (stūpa of Kaniṣka) at Sani monastery in Zanskar which has the hemi-spherical dome (aṇḍa) which is not the usual feature of chortens in Ladakh, also suggests through the tradition about Kushan evidence in the area, as also confirmed by the inscritpion of Vima Kadphises at Khalatse, which on one side towards south was connected with Kashmir and on the other with the route along the Indus through the difficult route along Zanskar, the river which joins Indus near Nimoo between Leh and Khalatse at a distance of about 34 km from Leh.

Interestingly, two stone slabs containing the famous Buddhist creed '*Ye dharma hetuprabhavā hetuṁ teshāṁ Tathāgatohyavadat, teshāṁ cha yo nirodho hyevam vādī Mahāśramaṇaḥ*' were found fixed on either side of the entrance of the main hall at Sani Monastery in Zanskar which were perhaps originally fixed along with such other slabs on the facade of the monastery where still a line of such inscribed slabs are visible. The writing suggests an early date of the monastery as also believed traditionally.

Francke, during his observations and study of skulls recovered from the Dard graves near Leh, has suggested that they belong to the early centuries of the Christian era between first to fifth centuries A D.[18] Apparently, the Dard nomads must have helped in the trade of the area which got impetus during the Kushan rule and much of the engravings on the boulders seemingly date back to the period and are located mainly on boulders near the camping grounds of ancient traders and their nomadic helpers.

Archaeologists from Germany and Pakistan under Karl Jettmar[19] and A.H. Dani[20] have explored a large number of sites on and around the Karakorum highway and have located numerous inscriptions in Brāhmī and Kharoṣṭhī, datable to the early centuries of Christian era and having names of Kushan emperors, kshatrapas, high officials and local rulers besides traders and monks along with human and animal figures and motifs engraved on boulders and rocks, many of which have similarity with those found in Ladakh. Geo-culturally the area comes under the same region as also most of these sites are located on the banks of Indus from Alam bridge in the north to Kohistan area in the south having important sites at Chilas, Thalpan Ziyarat, Hodar, Oshibat, Thor and Shatial. Towards north of Alam bridge where river Hunza meets the Indus such sites with rock engravings have been located on the banks of Hunza upto the place of the same name identified as Honosara (or Hanesara) Vishaya (district) by N.P. Chakravarti.[21]

Towards the close of the second phase of Darada activities the rock cut sculptures of Mulbekh, Apati, Kartse Khar, Sani, Drass, Hunder and Yansa are representative art works of the age. To this era belongs the group of buildings depicted in engravings which do not have the *aṇḍa* of a stūpa and have been identified at Chilas VII with cult buildings.[22]

The third phase has mostly engravings of Tibetan style of Chortens or stūpas, Tibetan inscriptions and figures of Buddha and minor deities in the typical Tibetan style which has very little affiliation with the Darada tradition which itself got defused in it in Ladakh. However, the second phase which continued till the ninth century A.D. provides much information about the folk rituals and tradition of the Daradas through the rock engravings found on thousands of boulders in the entire region. Various dance scenes, often in groups, cult-deities, ritualistic activities, symbols like footprints, palm-prints and other features of Dardic tradition and beliefs, Brāhmī and Kharoṣṭhī inscriptions mentioning local chieftains, traders, worshippers besides Kushan Kings and their figures, stūpas and material representation connected with both folk and classical forms, require their detailed study in understanding the life and activities of people inhabiting the region and those following their movements along the silk roads.

The West Iranian warrior with broad belt, fringed skirt and leggings, about to slaughter a goat or ibex represented on the Altar rock at Thalpan Bridge[23] and datable to the first millennium B.C. has a parallel at Tilichang in Ladakh engraved in the purely folk art tradition[24]. The folk deities also included Hāritī which is represented on a recess in the cliffs of Chilas II with Kharoṣṭhī label inscription and the folk tradition is further supported by a cult pillar to its left having human attributes[25]. The giant lady figure with legs apart and radiating lines on head at Chilas VI[26] belongs to the folk art of the early historic period. The tradition typical to the region depicting a chief or a deity seated on a throne who is offered a bowl by some people at Chilas II[27] or the enlightened one allowing a tigress having no milk for her cubs to devour him, a message of deepest compassion expressed through the tree nymph lamenting with the relatives at Chilas I[28] speak about the folk-lores developed from *Jātaka* stories popular among the Daradas and quite efficiently depicted in their artistic endeavour.

References

1. Philip Denwood, 'Temple and Rock Inscriptions at Alchi' in David L. Snellgrove and Tadeuz Skorupski, *The Cultural Heritage of Ladakh*, Vol. 2, New Delhi, 1979, pp. 117-164.
2. B.R. Mani, 'Rock Carvings and Engravings in Ladakh: New Discoveries', *Pragdhara*, Journal of the U.P. State Archaeology Department, No 9, Lucknow 1999, pp. 65ff.

3. Ved Kumari (ed). *The Nīlamata Purāṇa,* Vol. 1, Jammu, 1988, pp. 71-72.
4. John W. Mc Crindle, *Ancient India as Described in Classical Literature*, Reprinted, New Delhi, 1979, pp. 3, 51,198.
5. B.R. Mani, *op. cit.*
6. Giuseppe Tucci, 'On Swat, The Dards and Connected Problems' *East and West* Vol. 27, Nos 1-4, December 1977, Rome, p. 19.
7. Sanyukta Koshal, *Ploughhares of Gods-Ladakh-land Agriculture and Folk Tradition*, Vol I, New Delhi, 2001, pp. 558-61.
8. Sushma 'Saral', Laddakh Ke Lok Nritya' (in Hindi), *Hamara Sahitya 2002* (Ladakh issue), J&K Academy of Art, Culture & Languages, Jammu, 2002, p. 97.
9. Giuseppe Tucci, *op. cit*, p. 74.
10. R.S. Pandey (ed.) *Kalhaṇas Rājataranginī,* p. 87, IV. 169.
11. *Ibid*, p.137, V. 152.
12. *Indian Archaeology -1988-89—A Review*, p. 28
13. Karl Jettmar and Volker Thewalt, *Between Gandhāra and the Silk Roads*—Rock carvings along the Karakorum Highway, London, 1987, pls. 1 to 3.
14. A.H. Dani, *The Sacred Rock of Hunza, Journal of Central Asia*, Vol. VIII, No. 2, December, 1985, p. 7
15. Francke, A.H. *Antiquities of Indian Tibet*, Part I, Calcutta, 1914, pp. 95-96.
16. Vidula Jayaswal, *Kushana Clay Art of Gaṅgā Plains*, Delhi, 1991, pp. 44-45.
17. Mohammad Usman Hassan, Ras-Koh : At cross roads of Ancient Civilization', *South Asian Archaeology*, London, 1985, pp. 189-95.
18. A.H. Francke, *op. cit*, p. 74.
19. Karl Jettmar, *Zwischen Gandhara Und Den Seidenstrassen, Felsbilder am Karakorum Highway*. Entdechungen deutsch-Pakistanischer Expeditionen 1979-1984, Mainz am Rhein, 1985.
20. A.H. Dani, *Human Records on Karakorum Highway,* Islamabad, 1983; *Chilas the city of Nanga Parvat*, Islamabad, 1983; *The Sacred Rock of Hunza*, Islamabad 1985, p. 7.
21. N.P. Chakravarti, 'Hatun Rock Inscription of Patoladeva', *Epigraphia Indica*, Vol. XXX, 1953-54, pp. 227 and 230.
22. Herald Hauptmann (ed.), *The Indus Craddle and Crossroads of Civilization*, Islamabad, 1997, p. 46, Fig. 1.
23. Karl Jettmar and Volker Thewalt, *op. cit.*, pl. 5.

24. B.R. Mani, Op. cit., pl. 30
25. Karl Jettmar and Volker Thewalt, *op. cit.*, pl. 12.
26. *Ibid.,* pl. 22.
27. *Ibid.,* pl. 8.
28. *Ibid.,* fig. on p. 19.

8

Sirpur—The Grand Baleshwar Temple

—A.K. Sharma.

Sirpur (Lal-21° 25'N, Long 82° 11E) in district Mahasamund of Chhattisgarh state, India, a small village on the right bank of Mahanadi was once a large town of considerable importance. In fifth-eighth centuries A.D. Sirpur was the capital of Sarabhapuriyas and Panduvamsis of South Kosala. Its ancient name was 'Sripura'. As it contained a great number of dwelling houses, for all classes, king's palace, numerous temples and was situated in a forested country it was called 'pura', i.e. Sripura.

Urban development and city planning which developed during Harappan Period, the example of which are great cities like Mohenjodaro, Harappa, Lothal, Kalibangan, Rupar, Dholavira etc., survived during Early Historical period and later. In Dakshin Kosala (Chhattisgarh) the outstanding examples of are Sirpur, Malhar, Ratanpur etc. Out of these, so far, only Sirpur has been excavated on a large scale, giving a glimpse of city planning.

The selection of the site for their new capital by Sarabhapuriyas was strictly in accordance with the principles laiddown in *Vāstuśāstra*, about which two important works are *Mānsāra* and *Mayamatā Mayamata* belongs to Śaivasidhāntā is demonstrated by the leading place given to Śiva temples, by the chapter Liṅga and especially by the speculations on the nature of the Liṅga which it contains, and by the pantheon it describes which is essentially that is found in the *śaivāgma*.

The excavations at Sirpur have now proved with the unearthing of overwhelming number of Śiva temples housing four colours of Śiva lingas that Sirpur was basically

---

* After excavating Baleshwar temple complex, the author has recently excavated a huge Śiva temple with star-shaped garbh-griha at Mansar, Distt. Nagpur datable to 5th cent. A.D.

Fig. 9—Sirpur-Location map

planned as a *Śaivagama*. As *Mayamata* was not a sectarian work, it also details about forms of Viṣṇu, Buddha and Jina, and mentions about their temples which are not usual in *agamic* literature. Bruno Dagans correctly states. "It may be said, quite definitely, that the aim of the Mayamata is to organize the integration of the external manifestation of Siddhānta Śaivism in a context which could be qualified as "non-sectarian Hindu", so as to avoid the term 'secular which is not very appropriate when speaking of traditional India." And this "non-sectarian Hindu" aspect that prevailed at Sirpur during the rule of Sarabhapuriyas and Somavamsis have been proved by the excavations at Sirpur which has brought out Siva temples, Vishnu temples, Jina and Buddha viharas, all co-existing together.

It is at the selected site for the capital that Mahanadi meanders to North-east; the direction of the Gods, and flows for nearly 7 kms in this direction before turning to east. This meandering of the river sorrounds the capital city in half moon-shaped fashion in south-west and north-east whereas on the other half i.e. north-west, east and south-east, the area is enclosed by a chain of hills, nearly 4 kms away. In between the two half circles is the passage in the from of central furrow of barely seed, the two ends of which acted as entry and exist points to the capital.

Somavamshi king Nannadeva's son Teevardeva (grandson of Indrabal) captured Dakshin Kosala after defeating Sarbhapuriya king Mahapravar-raj as at this time we get Teevardeva's inscription from Sirpur and adjoining areas, in which Teevardeva has been described as ruler of entire Kosala (middle of 6th century A.D.). At this time Sirpur was in its Golden Era and reached the peak of glory. It is during this period that art, architecture, iconography and literature freely grew and Sirpur's fame spread to far off places.Probably it is due to this fame, Chinese traveller Huen-T'sang visited Sirpur in 639 A.D. He wrote that the inhabitants were tall, dark and prosperous. The king was Kshatriya and very benevolent. He discovered here as many as hundred Buddhist monasteries, inhabited by about-1000 monks, belonging to the *Mahayana* sect, and more than 150 temples.

The Buddhist association of Sirpur, suspected as early as 1881-82 by Cunningham on the basis of the find of a colossal head of Buddha and partly confirmed by the discovery of a complete inscribed image of Buddha in the first decade of the twentieth century and latest discovery of bronze images was borne out by the unearthing of two monasterise.[2]

Mahasivagupta Balarjuna's Lakshman temple stone incription says that his father Harshagupta was married to Sūryavarma's daughter Vasata. Sūryavarma was the son of Ishanvarma (551 A.D.)

Polamburin copper plate, "तिवर नगर भवन गतपरम युवति हृदय जन विहरण रति,"—

Vishnukundin King Madhav Varman I captured the entire Teevarnagar. As per prof. Mirashi, Teevarnagar was Teevardeva's capital and as such the time is middle of 6th cent. A.D. He has put Teevardeva's date as 560 A.D. This king's three incriptions found earlier are 1. Rajim copper plate, 2. Baloda copper plate and 3. Bonda copper plate. In 2002-2003 two large stone incriptions were discovered by the author during excavation of a lavishly carved Buddha Vihar with a huge monolithic Buddha image in *bhumi-sparsh mudra*. One of the stone incription has six partly visible and partly eroded lines. In the third line... वरदेव- Vardeva is clear. Before *Va* word the eroded word which is like 'ती' 'Tee' gives clear indiation of king Teevardeva of Sirpur.

The right half of another stone inscription discovered, in its fifth line gives the name श्री हर्ष Shri Harsha. This Harsha appears to be the son of Chandragupta, who was the brother of Teevardeva.

According to Pandit Lochan Prasad Pande[9]. Mahasivagupta Balarjuna's (son of Harshagupta and Vasata), Kingdom was spread upto Eastern seas (Dakshin Kosala, East Kosala, Toshal, Utkal and Odra (ओड्र). In Lakshman temple inscription Harshagupta has been described as Prak-Parameshwara (प्राक्-परमेश्वर). In Lodhia copper plate Balarjuna has been described as Tri Kalingadhipati. (त्रिकालिंगाधिपति), This was issued in the 57th year of his rule. He ruled from 595 to 650 A.D., for nearly 60 years. According to D.C. Sircar, either Balarjuna or his successor was defeated by Chalukya King Pulkeshin II. In Pulkeshin II's Aihole incription it is said that he was the monarch of entire Dakshin Path and his kingdom spread upto Narmada. According to Bilhari inscription, son of Kalchuri King Kokkat, Mugdhatung snatched Pali from Kosala king. Inscription of Nala king Vilastung, found at Rajim also indicates in this direction. Ratanpur inscription of Kalchuri king Jajjaldev I made Tuman as his capital and Dakshin Kosala came under his domain. Dr. M.G. Dikshit got 106 Kalchuri coins in Sirpur excavations. Similarly he got structural remains of Period II which are of Kalchuri period. It appears that after Balarjuna Sirpur got neglected and lost its capital status.

The excavations by Dr. M.G. Dixit, in the habitation area has revealed three periods of occupation during Early Historical times.Period I dates back to the last quarter of the 5th cent A.D. as indicated by a fragmentary gold coin of king Prasannamatra of the Sarabhapura dynasty. Period II dates back to sixty-eight century A.D. This period of Panduvamsi dynasty witnessed large scale structural activity, attested to by several brick and stone temples (majority are Śiva temples), Buddhist monasteries, palace complex, priest's houses and attached water tanks. Period III attributed to the eleventh century A.D. and after, is datable to the Kalachuri dynasty of Ratanpur branch. It comprises of structures built by re-using maternal mostly of the earlier periods.

SIRPUR-2004 DISTT.-MAHASAMUND, CHHATTISGARH

PLAN OF MAHASIVAGUPTA BALARJUNS RESIDENCE, SRP-6

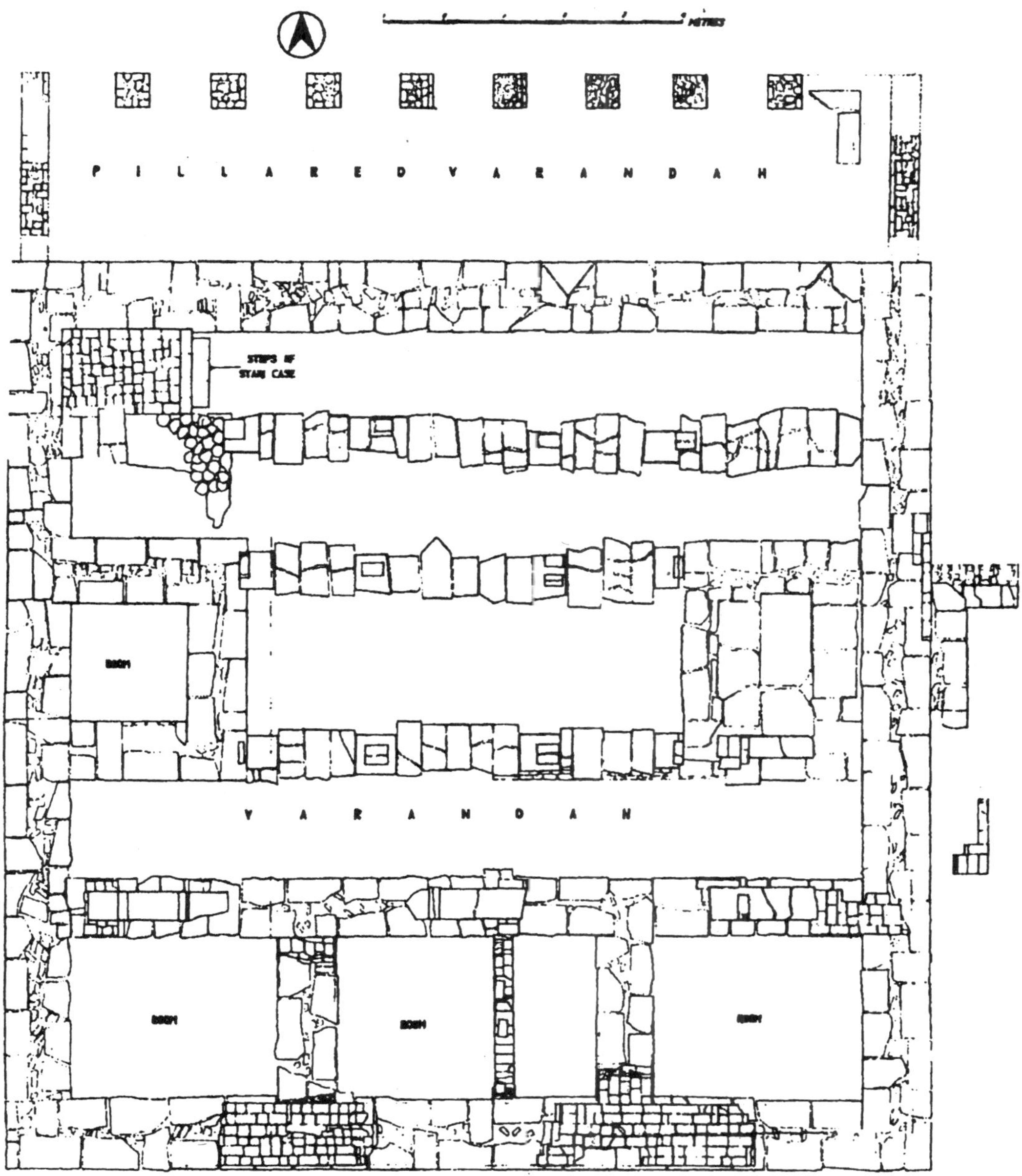

Fig. 10-Sripur-Maha Sivagupta Balarjuna's Residence (SRP-6)

The present excavations which began in 2000 A.D. have so far brought to light,eight Śiva temples, a *tantric* temple, four Buddha Vihara complexes, a sprawling palace complex, a chieftain's residence Fig 10, six residences of priests and a modest residence of Maha Śivagupta Balarjuna, meant for religious occasions, in the *Pancayatana* Śiva temple complex P1 IIA. From one of the rooms of his residence, a seal with the inscription 'Śivagupta-rajas' in 7th Cent. A.D. Brahmi was recovered (Pl.IIB). Before God the king never prefixed word 'Maha'.

All Buddha viharas and residential complexes, including the palace are two storeyed structures, top story approached by flight of steps and topped by stone slabs and always either in the west or south and inside the building. All the buildings have stocks of lime lump stored in huge conical red earthen jar (*Nanda*) for white washing the lime plastered buildings, on religious and festive occasions. Every priest's, house and also the chieftain's, house has a store room (*Bhandar Griha*) located to the south west or west of the building. It has no doors. It was approached fron top, as is the pracice in Chhattisgarh villages even to this day. All the priest's houses, so far excavated, are located to the south of the temple and further to the south of these residences a modest size tank is located which, as per evidences show that these tanks were multifunctional including for irrigation.

The Brahmānical association of Sirpur, teeming with beauliful temples, including the famous Lakshamana temple, was long known.

In 2003-03 a huge, mound in the centre of the village was excavated, as few years back a hoard of copper plates of the period of Mahasivagupta Balarjuna, were recovered from near his modest residence, located south of the complex.

Though the site has been badly plundred, since decades, by the villagers, by careful excavation, plan of a *Pañcāyatana* (quincunux type) Śiva temple complex has been brought to light (PI. IIIA). It comprises of two large *yūgal* temples P1 IIIB, sorrounded on four corners with four smaller Śiva temples, a priest's house Just to the south-west of the southern main temple, king's residence south of the main southern temple and a huge *nagna tadāga* (Water tank) further to the south of the king's residence.

In the Suranga Teela Pañcāyatana complex which is under excavation, the joining method used for joining two dressed block of stones is iron dowels. In the Baleshwar temple complex and in other residential buildings and Buddh Viharas etc. the binding material used is in the form of well shieved paste, the details of which we find in *Mayamatam* (मयमतम) vol. I–

92. करालमुद्गी गुल्माषकल्कचिक्कणसाह्वया:
चूर्णोपयुक्ता: पञ्चैते सर्वकर्मसनातना:।

Karāla, *mudgi*, *gulmāsa*, *kalka*, and *Cikkana*, mixed with lime are, all five, suitable for every kind of work.

96. पूर्वोक्तमात्रसिकताचणकश्चूर्णमानतः।
क्रियार्थं प्रेषितं कल्कं चिक्कणमस्तु केवलम्।।

To make *Kalka*, grain of sand of the dimension indicated above and (morsels) of line the size of a Chickpea should be crushed together. *Cikkaṇa* must be homogenous (liquid).

97. निश्छिद्रमिष्टमानेन गोयमिष्टकया दृढ़म्।
पूर्वोक्तानां च पञ्चानां विधांतव्यं पृथक पृथक।।

98(a). तत्र तत्र तदुत्तेन प्रव्येण परिकल्पयेत्।

98(b). केवलेनाम्भसा पूर्वं पूर्वांस्त्रिस्त्रिः प्रकुट्टयेत्।।

97-98 (a) These five products are used seperatly to join bricks securely together without gaps and as prescribed; the proper one should be chosen for each usage.

98 (b) First, each of the above (substances) is crushed with pure water.

101. कल्कं च चिक्क्णं तेन कल्कनीयं विच्क्षणैः
दधिदुग्धमाषयूषगुडाज्यक दलीफलैः।।

101 (a) They are ground anew with sap from Kṣīradruma, *Kadamba*, mango, *abhaya* and *akṣa* as well as with juice of the fruits of the three myrobolans and water of broadbean; next, after the gravel, shelly and lime have been mixed with well water, the mixture should be pounded by horses hooves, then filtered through fine linen, this is how well advised people impart viscocity to *Kalka* and *Cikkana*.

102. जलैश्च नालिकेरस्य चूतपक्वरसैः सह।
कल्पितं शिल्पिभिर्यत् तद् बन्धोदकभिति स्मृतम्।।

103. शुद्धिं शुद्धोदकेनादौ कृत्वा बन्धाम्भसा ततः।
अलिप्य सुधया कार्या नानारूपन्वितक्रिया।।

101(b)-103. That called *bandhodaka* is prepared by the masons, using curd, milk, bean water, molasses, clarified butter, bananas, coconut milk and mango juice. After the wall has been washed with clear water the *bandhodaka* is used as a coating if images of any sort are to be placed there.

Pañcāyatana type of temple complex developed around 6th cent. A.D. Inspite of large scale destruction, plan of two twin main temples in the centre Figs. (11-14) and three sub-shrines in north-east, south-west (P1, Fig IVA 15,16) and north west

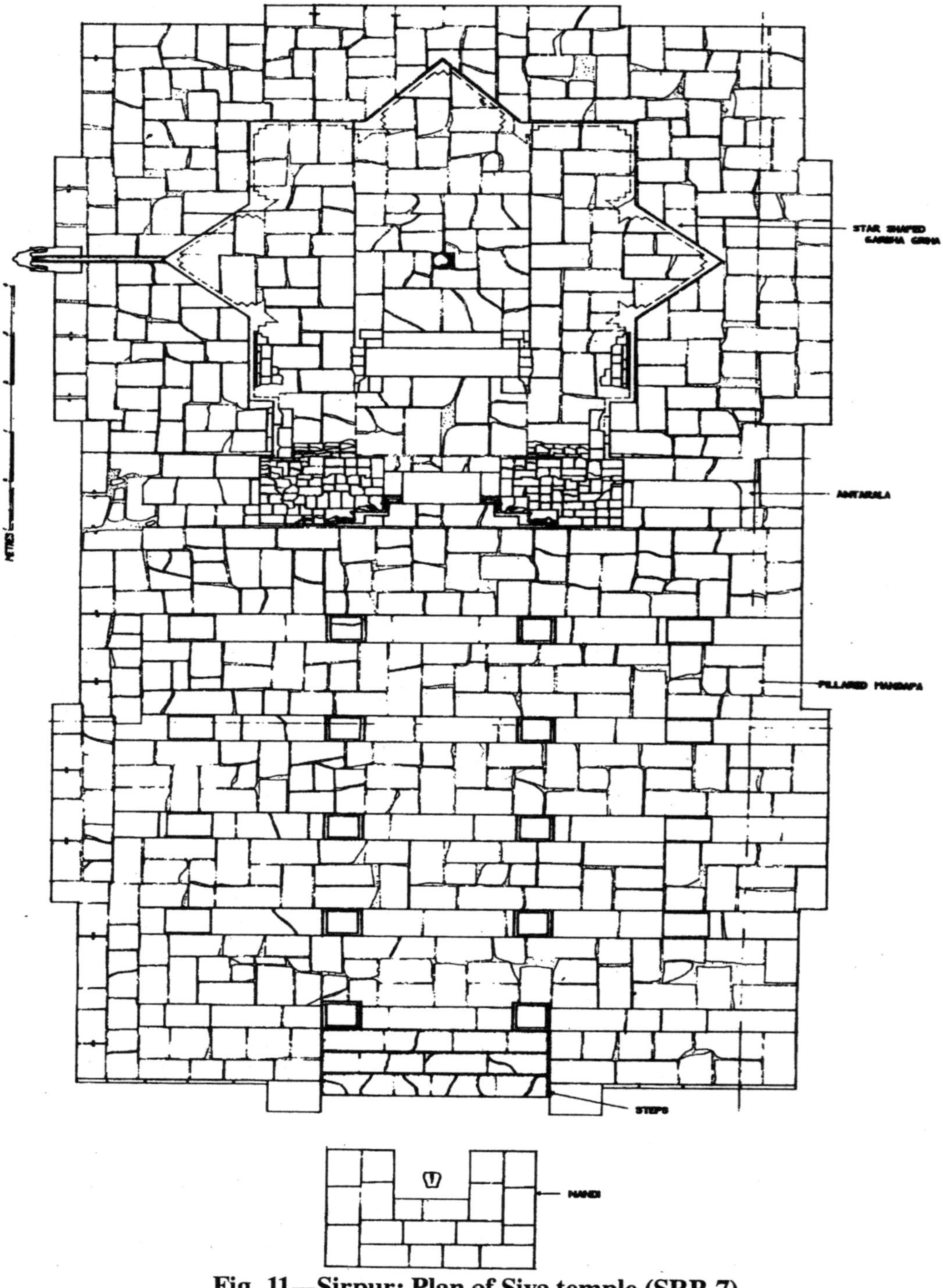

Fig. 11—Sirpur: Plan of Siva temple (SRP-7)

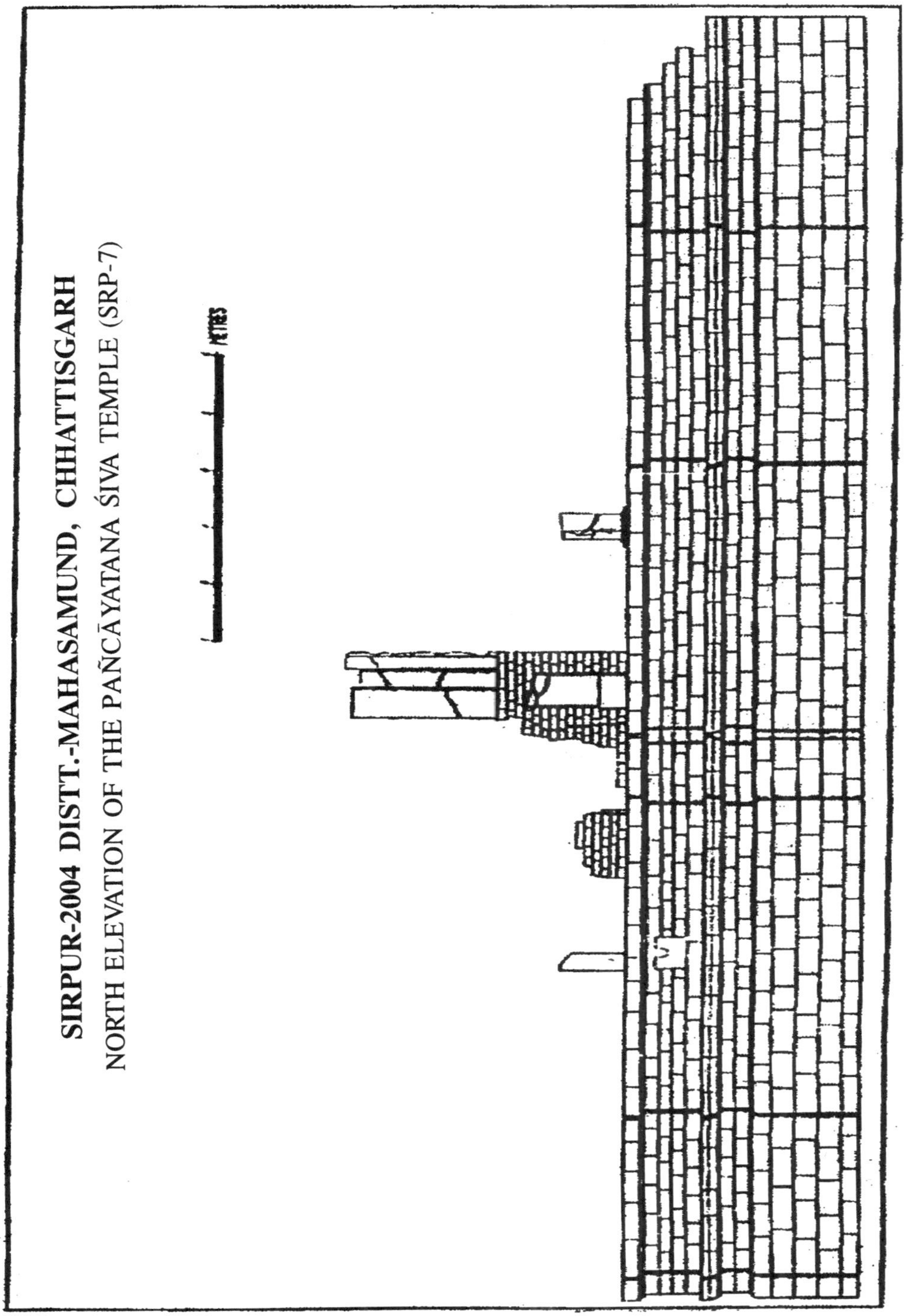

Fig. 12—Northern Elevation of Siva temple (SRP-7)

SIRPUR-2004 DISTT.-MAHASAMUND, CHHATTISGARH

PLAN OF THE PAÑCĀYATANA ŚIVA TEMPLE (SRP-8)

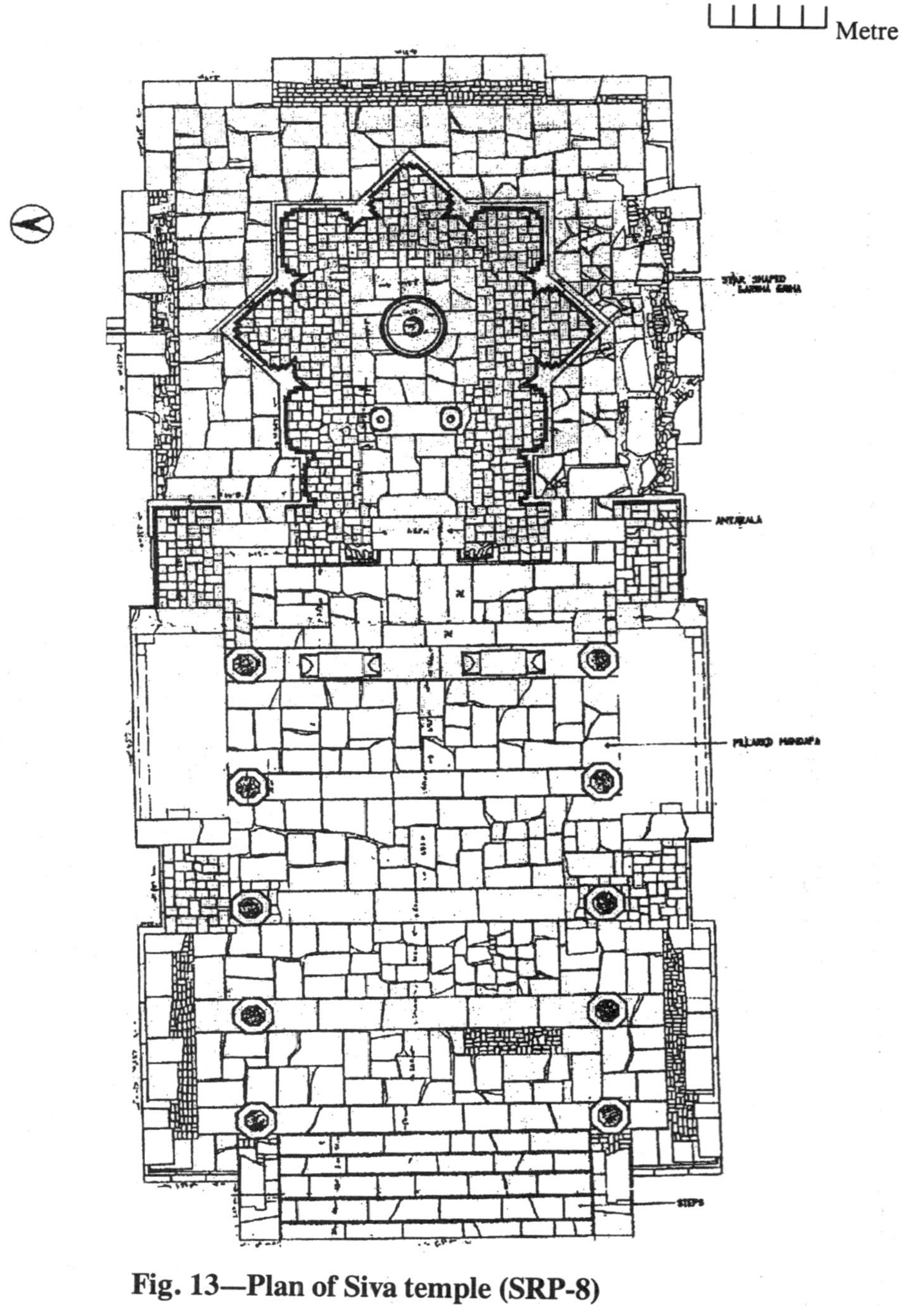

Fig. 13—Plan of Siva temple (SRP-8)

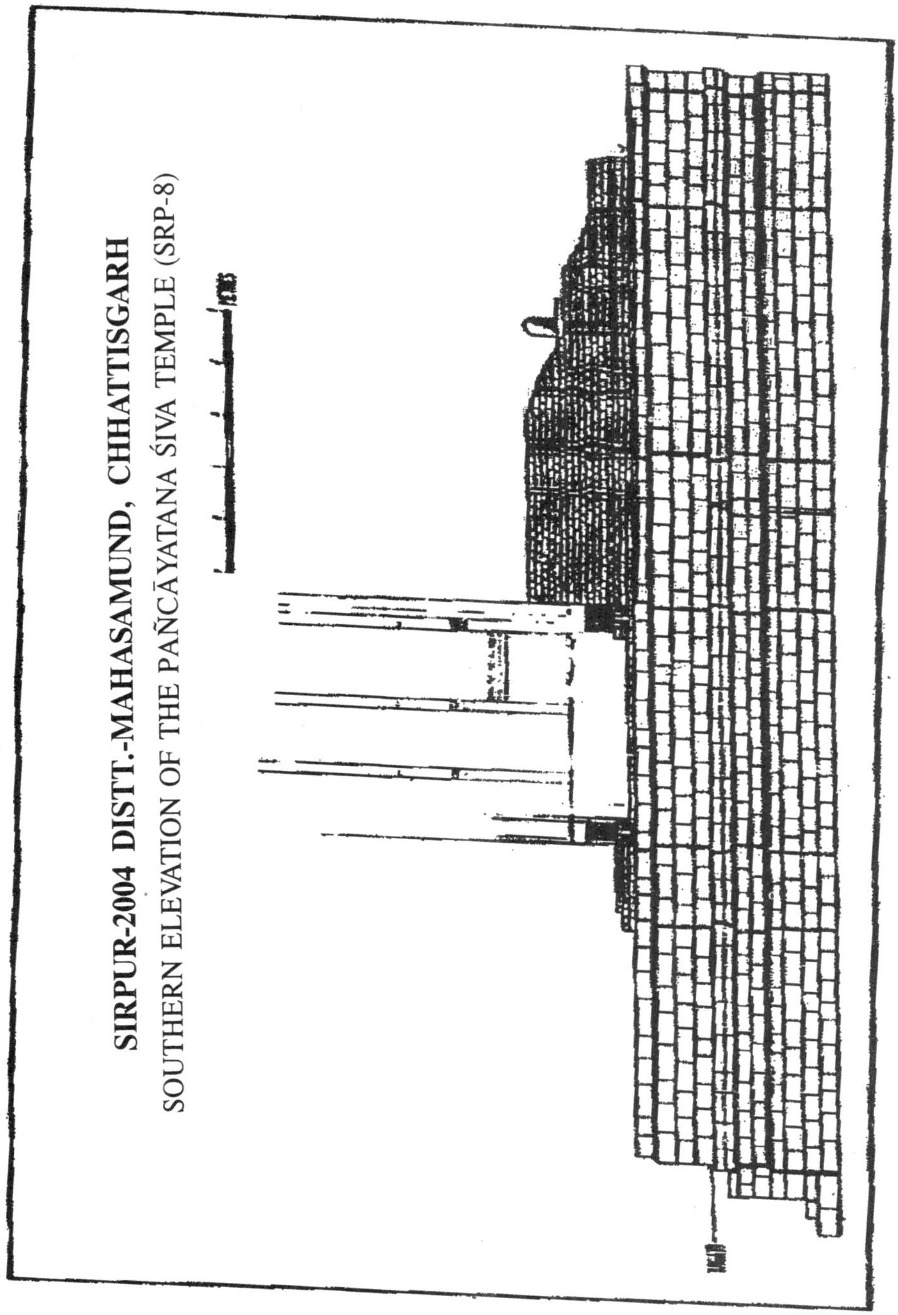

Fig. 14—Southern elevation of Siva Temple (SRP-8)

SIRPUR-2004 DISTT.-MAHASAMUND, CHHATTISGARH

PLAN OF THE PANCAYATANA SIVA TEMPLE (SRP-9)

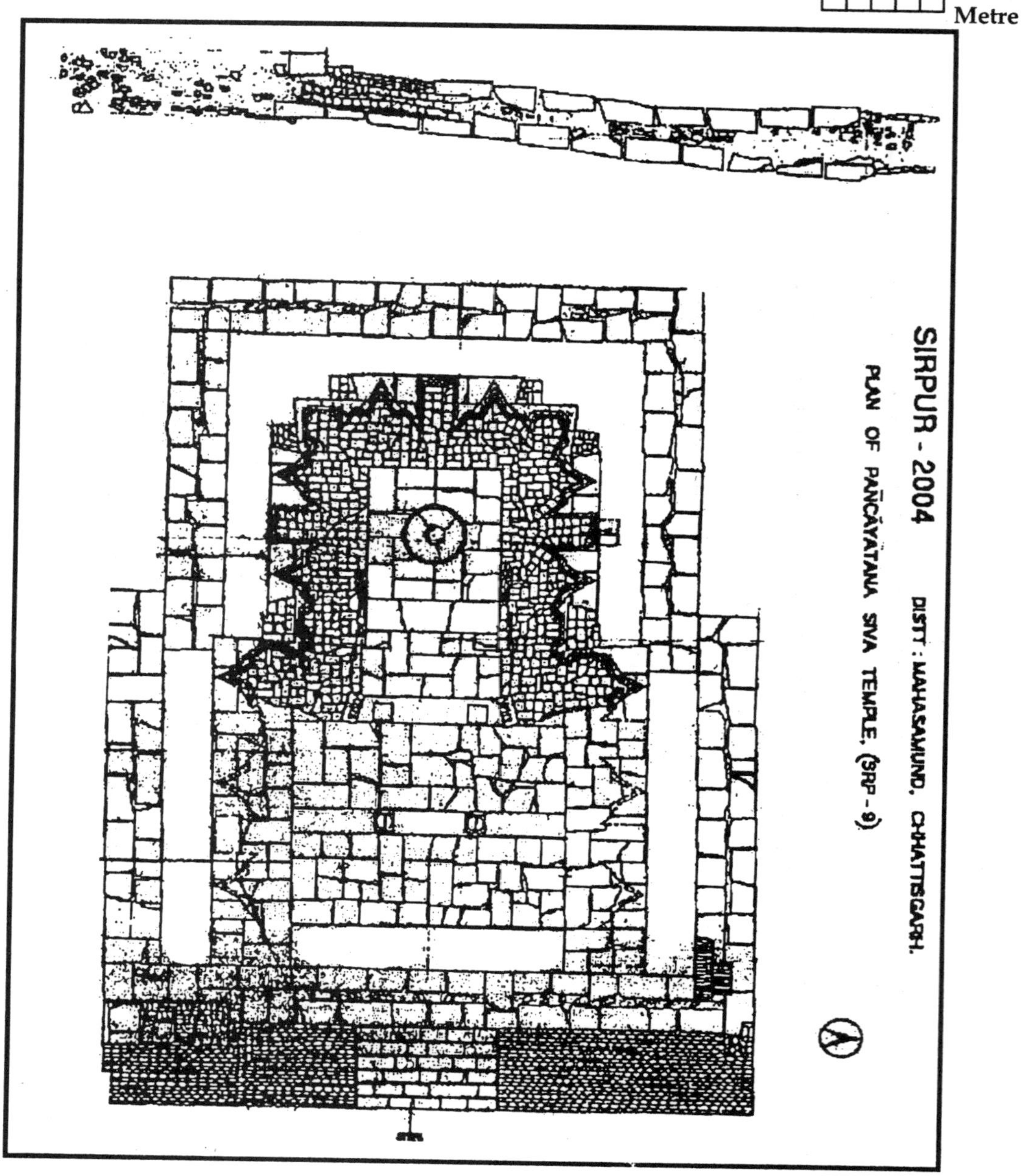

Fig. 15-Plan of Siva Temple (SRP-9)

SIRPUR-2004 DISTT.-MAHASAMUND, CHHATTISGARH

NORTHERN ELEVATION OF THE PAÑCĀYATANA ŚIVA TEMPLE (SRP-9)

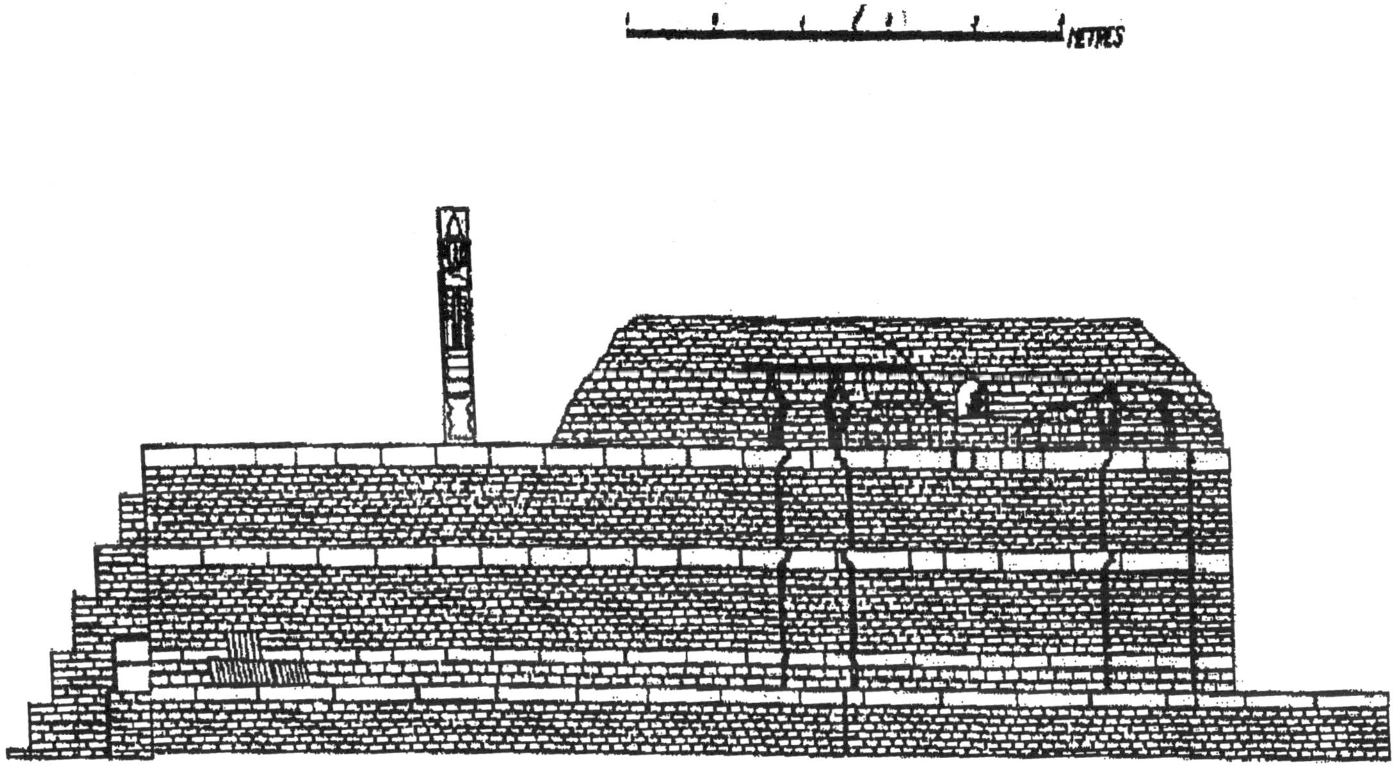

Fig. 16—Sirpur-Elevation of Śiva Temple (SRP-9)

could be exposed. The entire complex was fortified with 1.0 metres wide stone and brick wall, traces of which to a length of 20 metres could be exposed in the west only.

The central ones and the one in the south-west corner stood on lofty moulded terraces (*Jagati*) of Cuddapa blocks brought form a distance of nearly 70 kms. east. This stone quarry between Mahanadi and Mand river, near the famous piligrim centre of Sheorinarayan, is still alive. The *Jagati* is relieved with niches and is approached by a flight of steps (*sopanas*) on the west as the *yugal* temples face west towards the river (Pl IVB). The two subsidiary shrines on south-west and north-west face east, while the third in south-east faces west.

Remains only upto Jagati portion and traces of super structures, particularly of *garbha-gṛha* and *antarāla*, made of moulded burnt bricks could be found. The layout is in accordance with the description in the *Haryasirsapañcaratā* as well as in the *Agni Purana*. The two central temples, in north and south, elongated on plan, measure 22.0x9.20m and 22.0x 10.50m. respectively.

The *adhiṣṭhānas* of main temples comprise of 13 extent courses of well cut stone blocks. While the 9.20 wide north-south wall is plain, the 22.0m long east-west axis has projection and 40 cm. deep recessions alternately. Begining from east i.e. from *garbha-gṛha* end the first recession is 2.10m long followed by 4.75m projection, then 2.75m. recession followed by 4.60m.. projection, 1.70m recession again 4.60m. prejection and finally 1.50m deep recession which is 1.10m. ṁ length.

The *garbha-gṛha* of both the main temples is star-shaped on plan (Pl. VA), on the exterior*, while rectangular from inside. Each star has five rays, with each ray measuring 1.40m ṁ length. The two basal straight arms of the star also measure 1.40m ṁ length, each. The interior rectangular *garbha-gṛhas* measure 3.30m (north-south) x 2.20m. (east-west) with a 1.55m. wide entrance. All the three temples house huge white Śiva lingas, measuring 1.05m. in height, each, with their components, square *Brahmā bhaga*, octogonal *Viṣṇu bhaga* and cylindrical *Rudra bhaga* of equal size i.e. 35.cm. in height and 35 cm. in girth each. They have Vishnu Sutra engraved on the front face with a 13.5cm. linga engraved below top loop of Vishnu Sutra. The lingas are placed on a square socketed pedestal measuring 36.0x36.0cm. in the centre of the *garbha gṛha*, to the left of the line that passes through its exact centre, so that they are slightly displaced towards the north-east.

The linga is mounted on a square pedestal which has nine circular holes, one bigger hole in the centre sorrounded by 8 smaller holes of equal size at equidistance, depiction of *Nava-grahas* (Pl. VB). The square *Brahmā bhaga* is firmly fitted in the square socket of the pedestal. The three piece white *yoni peeth*, 62.0cm. in height and 1.25m. in girth is placed Just below the *Rudra bhaga*. It has a 8 cm. wide *pranala* which runs to north and ends in a *makara-mukha* at the fringe of the *adhiṣṭhāna* wall.

In front of the *garbha-gṛha* is the *antarala* which is 1.55m. in width and is capped by 45cm. wide laterite stone slabs. On the entrance of the *antarāla* stand the tall figures of the sacred river Goddesses, the Gaṅgā and the Yamunā, standing on their vehicles (*Vāhana*), crocodile and tortise (*Kurma*), respectively (Pl. VIA). The *grabha-gṛha* is entered through a *sankh-dwara*, made of huge laterite blocks and uprights.

The two main temples had pillared halls (*mahā-maṇḍapa*), in front of the main sanctum. In case of southern one it had ten monolithic octogonal pillars, resting on square bases. Each pillar is 1.55m. in girth. The *maṇḍapa* is divided into five open segments, each having two pillars kept at a distance of 5.55m. The segments are 6.60m in length and 1.70m. in width, each. In between the two rows of pillars there is 65cm. wide base wall of rectangular cut shale stones, to give strength to the *maṇḍapa* floor. Below the base of pillars there runs a row of laterite stone slabs whereas the segments are floored with white stones. The two side walls of *maṇḍapa* are 1.40m wide.

The northern main temple had sixteen circular monolithic pillars resting on octogonal bases. The south-western shrine had a *maṇḍpa* resting on four pillars.

It appears the temples harboured *bhadra-devas* in the principle niches (*bhadra khatakas*) as many such huge sculptures in badly mutilated condition were recovered. Mention may be made of Mahisasurmardini, Yama, Sūrya and Kartikeya riding on three peacocks (Pl VIB), which is of rare occurance. The dolomite carved uprights on the two sides of the northern temple, in the *maṇḍapa* region, held images, also carved on dolomite blocks. The horizontal and vertical bars had carved chaitya-arches where as the sculptures were held by inserting in square or rectangular sockets in the horizontal bars. The sculptures are mostly of imperial persons and mithuna figures, dancing damsels, quarrel scenes amongst the two wives of Mahasivagupta Balarjuna, named Amra Devi and Ambaddi Devi. Amra Devi was from Chhattisgarh whereas Ambaddi Devi was either from Andhra Pradesh or from Karnataka. The ruler himself has been shown dancing with his two queens, in a temple. The most remarkable figures are those depictiñg the monarch hiding between the two wives, when they are bitterly quarreling, snatching each others hairs or hitting with their legs. The expression of helplessness of the king has been masterly captured on such a hard stone. The roaring lion figures with full erect male organs. is a master piece in dileneation, expression and anatomical details (Pl VIIA).

As both obverse and reverse of the sculptures are carved, it is clear that they served as running pannels in the *maṇḍapa*, so that they could be viewed both from inside and outside.

In front of the southern main temple, nearly 2.0m west of the steps a rectangular

Nandi shrine, built of cuddapah blocks could be located in extremely damaged condition. Only fregments of *Nandi* could be found in the debris.

The decoralive fragments of ceilings of *mahāmaṇḍapa* or *sabhamaṇḍapa*, recovered indicate that the temples were of *samtala* variety adorned with full- bloom lotuses.

Another Śiva temple with star-shaped *garbha-gṛha* was exposed and conserved to the south-west of Anand Prabhu Kutī vihar. This temple on plan resembles Siddesvara temple at Palari in Raipur district, Chhattisgarh. The Śiva temple at Adbhar in district Champa—Janjgir, Chhattisgarh originally consisted of a sanctum, *antarāla*, *maṇḍapa* and *mukhamaṇḍapa*. Its *garbha-gṛha* is star-shaped. The twin temples at Sirpur resemble on plan the Dhobini Śiva temple located in Bilaspur district of Chhattisgarh, which has been assigned to c. A.D. 700-725. These temples in Chhattisgarh, with star-shaped *garbha-gṛha* are earlier to those is Central india.

The priest's house on the south-western corner of the southern main temple is north-facing and is a modest building. In front is the four pillared verandah measuring 6.50×1.90m. The pillars are 40x30cm. There is a 0.95 ×1.90m platform on the western corner of the verandah. After the verandah there is a single hall measuring 6.0 ×2.50m. The brick walls with stone foundation are 65cm. in thickness. Room, verandah and platform have stone floorings.

Balarjuna's house is a north facing double storeyed building, on plan measuring 15.50m. (east-west) x15.0m.(north-south). Upto plinth level the foundation is of laterite and shale blocks, whereas the super structure was of bricks.Ground floor has sixteen rooms measuring 4.40x2.60m, each facing a long east-west verandah measuring 13.30x1.50m. The house is entered through a pillared verandah measure 13.30x2.60m. The pillars appear to be of bricks. The stair-case with stone flooring is in the central verandah on the western corner. It is raised on a 2.30x2.30m. platform. Below the stair case are stacked lumps of lime. From the eastern side also, on the north-eastern corner, there is another entrance. The door uprights are of laterite blocks and had a single fly door each as evidenced by presence of single door sockets (Fig, Pl. IIA).

The entire complex had stone flooring. From the residence of Balarjuna a noteworthy find is the iron face mask and halmet. The halmet is made of superior quality iron as it has hardly rusted in last 1500 years.

Nearly 300m west of this temple complex is located the tallest and biggest temple complex of Sirpur, named locally as Suranga Teela complex.

The layout of the structural remains, so for exposed at Sirpur show that all the buildings including the religious ones were constructed strictly following the Vāstuśāstra norms and parallel to the main current of river Mahanadi. Sirpur was laid on *Swastika nagari* plan. It follows a *swastika* figure and comprises of four main streets. The centre of the *swastika* is occupied by a lofty *Pañcāyatana* Śiva temple raised on a 5.10 m dressed stone *adhiṣṭhana* (highest in Dakshin Kosala).

Aclonowledgements

I am thankful to the Director General, Archaeological Survey of India for granting licence to excavate at Sirpur, a centrally protected site. Excavations were conducted on behalf of Bodhisatva Nagarjuna Smarak Sanstha Va Anusandhan Kendra, Nagpur whose president, Arya Nagarjuna Surai Sasai, took keen interest. I am beholden to Shri Jagat-Pali. Joshi, Retd. Director General,A.S.I. for his guidance as co-excavator, My grateful thanks are due to Shri J.S. Dubey, Senior Draftsman and Ku. Swati Gaikwad, Senior Artist for the drawings, Ku. Shilpa Rangari, and Shri Praveen for their untiring help during excavations.

References

1. *Archaeological Survey of India*, *Report*, Vol. VII, Delhi, 1878.
2. *Archaeological Survey of India*, *Reports*- I-XXIII- 1862-1885.
3. *Indian Archaeology*-1953-54—A *Review*, New Delhi.
4. *Indian Archaeology*- 1954-55—A. *Review*, New Delhi.
5. *Pura-ratna, Emerging Trends in Archaeology, Art, Anthropology, Conservation and History*, (eds.) C. Margabandhu, A.K.Sharma, et. al., vol.III, New Delhi-2002.
6. Falk, Reitz, Berlin, Germany, *World Archaeology Congress*-3, New Delhi,1994.
7. D. Barrelt and M.G. Dikshit, *Mukhalingam Temples, Sirpur and Rajim Temples*, Bombay, 1960.
8. Krishna Deva, *Temples of india*, New Delhi, 1995.
9. Lochan Prasad Pandeo, *Mahakoshal Historical Society papers*, vols. 1 and 2.
10. Mishra, P.L., *Dakshin Kosala ka Prachin Itihas*, (Hindi), Raipur, 2003.
11. Srivastava, Mahesh Chandra, *Sirpur* (Hindi), Bhopal, 1984.
12. Central Provinces, District Gazetteers, Raipur District, 1909.
13. Bruno DAGENS, *Mayamata*—An Indian Trealise on Housing Architecture and Iconography, New Delhi—1985, pp. iv-v.
14. Bruno DAGENS, *Mayamatam* (मयमतम्)-Trealise of Housing, Architecture and Iconography, (Sanskrit-Text edited and translated by Bruno DAGENS) Indira Gandhi National Centre for the Arts, New Delhi, 1994, pp. 275-277.

9

Punjeri—A Megalithic Site in Kanchipuram Dist.

—*Capt. H. Barnes**

The brief report which follows describes an unexcavated megalithie site with sarcophagi which came to light in August 2004 owing to quarrying of red soil at Punjeri which is a known urn burial site near Mamallapuram also known as Mahabalipuram in Kanchipuram District. This region is famous for its megalithic sites.

The megalithic sites in Kanchipuram District of Tamilnadu were explored between 1944 and 1948. Some notable megalithic sites like Sanur, Pallavaram, Kunnattur and Amrithalingam were excavated between 1950-55 where besides the usual megalithic materials, several sarcophagi were reported. At Punjeri, besides urns, four partially exposed sarcophagi are seen besides probably others still buried. (as shown in the photographs). The megalithic sites at Pallavaram, Kunnattur and Punjeri are nearly on the same longitude ie. 80° 10'E and there is some similarity in the sarcophagi too. A sketch showing comparison is attached.

The Site:

Punjeri lies less than 2 kms from Mamallapuram which is also known as Mahabalipuram. The site measuring approx. 400 x150 meters on approx 12°37'N Latitude and 80° 11'E longitude is in Tirukkalukkunram taluk of Kanchipuram District and consists of four small granitic rocky outcrops on the western bank of an estuary. Small abandoned stone quarries, disturbed boulders, foliated rocks, barrows, partially exposed urns and sarcophagi in red stony soil are seen on the western side of the site while the eastern side has urn burials in light brown sandy soil. A disused track runs north-south through the site. The southern and eastern sides of the granitic out-

---

* *Security Officer, Archaeological Survey of India, Chennai Circle, Chennai.*

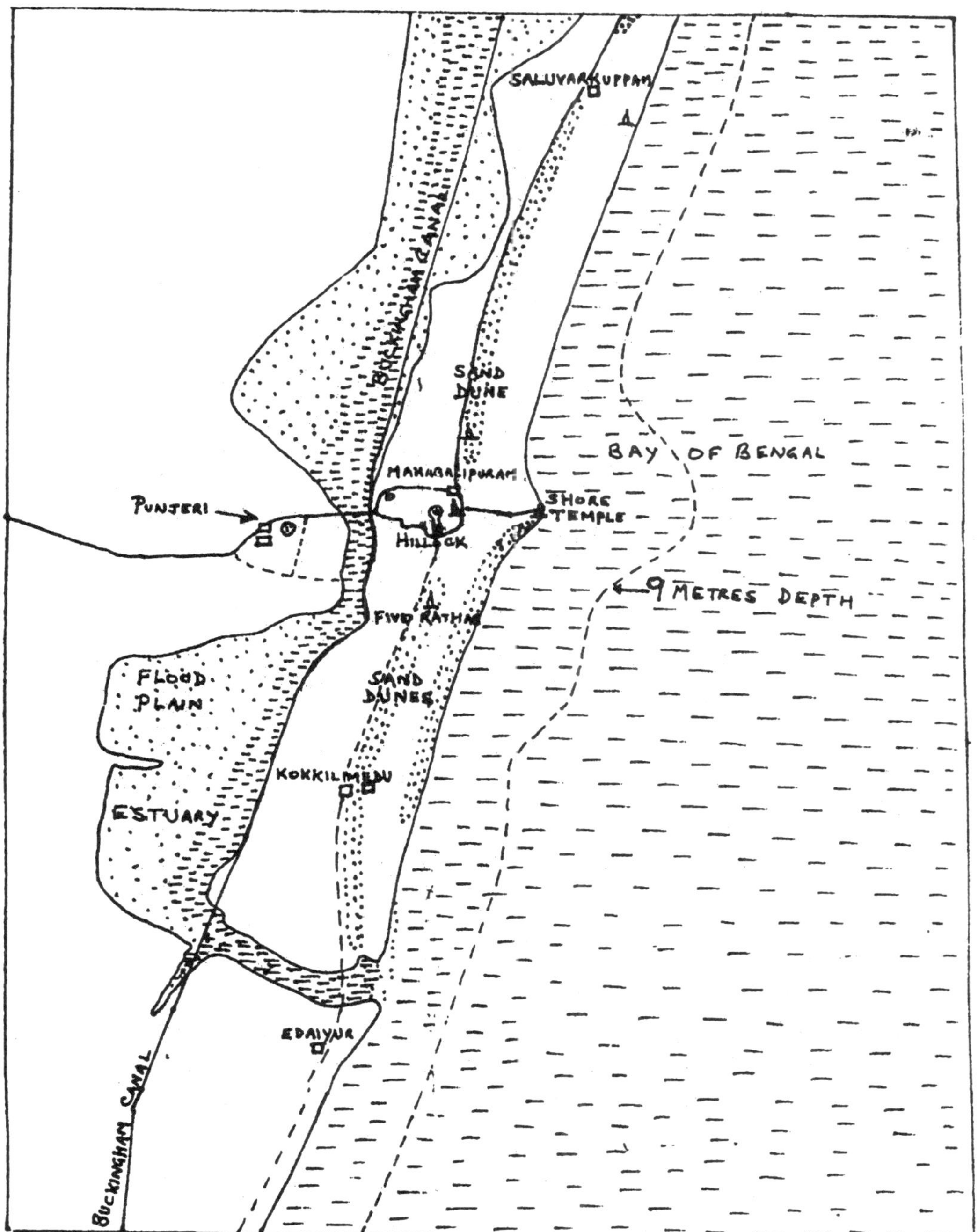

Fig. 17 : Sketch Showing Punjeri, Mamallapuram and its Environs

crops had been quarried for soil, thus creating a cutting and exposing some sarcophagi and urns. Moreover stone quarrying also has been done nearby. The sarcophagi are in a battered condition. Earthquakes or perhaps detonation waves during quarrying could have shattered the buried material. The embankment is collapsing gradually and the surface is littered with pottery, stones and other material.A socketed arrowhead and pieces of a curved blade of iron were found from one sarcophagus. Two crude microliths were found on the northern end of the site. Other materials found are thick, reddish painted pieces of sarcophagi rims with chain-like decoration, thick pieces of terracota with holos, Black and Red Ware and iron pieces. The sarcophagi appear to be of two types—one a robust looking domed one and the other flatter and shallower. One has a partially broken granite slab flush on it. Strangely, some roundish pebbles buried here seem to have an outer layer which resembles stony pottery. The orientation of the burials seems radial or semi-circular generally facing east. Some of the rocks and stones here are ferruginous and contain enough iron ore, so as to be picked up with a magnet. Sarcophagi, may be new here and the burials seem to be elaborate and customary.

Use of Iron:

Iron Industry followed by native may have developed here. Besides the ore other necessary local material like charcoal, sand, water, clay wood etc. are easily available and the making of furnaces and the processes were very simple and could be done wherever ore was available. A brief account of the local method of making iron and steel on the east coast as mentioned in a British period manual is given for its importance. The ore which is locally available in this region and known as 'canacull' is collected, broken, washed and then heated in an earthen furnace which is like a lime kiln but has two bellows of entire goat skins. The earthen furnace is filled at the bottom with charcoal. Then ore moistened with water is placed on it. Several layers are thus placed. Then the fire is lit and the bellow worked for about three hours. Then the iron is taken out with tongs and hammered to free it from the dross. This iron is reddish and brittle. To make steel, small crucibles of mixed, very fine clay and rice husks are prepared. Into these crucible iron pieces 25% and wood pieces 75% of wild cinnamon bush (*Gassia auriculata*) and few leaves of celandine (*Asclepia gigantia*) are filled. An earthern lid is put on the mouth and sealed. Several such crucibles of about 20cms diameter are placed in a furnace and covered with charcoal. The furnace is approximatly half meter square & 1.5 meter high. The furnace is lit and the bellows worked for about three hours. After this the furnace is allowed to cool and the steel extracted. This native steel was well known to Persians also since ancient times who praised it. Iron imported from India also went into the making of Damascus steel swords.

Geography:

The site Punjeri lies in an area which slopes from west to east and forms a peninsula with high ground towards west and the bed and flood plain of the estuary on the other three sides. This estuary joins the sea about four kms. south of Punjeri. The eastern horizon is dominated by the hillock and lighthouse at Mamallapuram. In fact a line drawn due east along the parallel from Punjeri passes over hillock and towards shore temple which is further west. Here also the slope of the land from hillock to the shore temple is west to east. If we proceed offshore eastward, there is a promontory-like ground just off the shore where the depth of the sea is shallower. The depth of the sea east of shore temple as shown in a century old map is about 9 meters upto a distance of 1500 m East. (Lat. 12° 6'50" N & Long 80° 12'50"E). The shore line runs roughly in a NNE-SSW direction. On the northern shore the samc depth is closer to the shore at lat. 12°37'50"N and long 80°12'30"E. On the southern shore this depth extends to a distance of 800m east on lat 12°36'30" N and long. 80°12'15"E. The 75m depth contour off Chennai lies at 16km east and at 18 im at Pondichsrry, while at Mamallapuram it lies 30 kms east. If the sea level were lower, this area east of the shore temple would form a rocky promontary. This local topography of the sea is probably responsible for the formation of sand dunes here and also for lessening the impact of the Tsunami on Dec.04. Another notable feature of the coastline are long, low & narrow sand dunes between 30-50m wide and about 3m high. One dune in this area runs NNE to SSW from Muttukandu (12°50'N) north of Kovalam to Kokkilimedu (12°35'35") where it turns due southward and ends at the mouth of the estuary. (12°34'30"N). The distance of this dune from the sea shore varies from 300m to 600m. The tiger cave and Cave temple at Saluvankuppam (4km north of Mamallapuram) and Mukundanayanar temple on the northern boundary of Mamallapuram village are located on this dune. The plinths (bases) of these monuments are about 3 m below the surface of the dune. Similarly the five rathas located on the southern side of Mamallapuram are also on this sand dune. Another smaller sand dune which is about 3 kms in length runs right on the shore, from the shore temple to the south east of Kokkilimedu. It was this dune that was recently eroded by the Tsunami in December 2004 exposing several carved sacrificial rocks and other structures on the southern side of the shore temple complex. From the above it seems that the sand dunes have been forming since these monuments were completed. This also may have silted up any dockyards and channels then existing at Mamallapuram and Punjeri. Moreover, the Palar river which now joins the sea at Edaiyur may have had the southern part of its delta at Mamallapuram in Pre-historic times when wetter climate would have favoured thick vegetation and a variety of fauna which have been depicted in the carvings here. The land west the sea shore in this area is generally low lying with many irrigation tanks and rocky knolls. The symbolic role of the five elements i.e. Earth, Water, Fire,

Air and Ether are represented, especially the first three with three and five-celled temples. A five celled rock cut cave on the hillock faces west towards Punjeri. A three celled rock cut cave temple on the sea shore at Saluvankuppam has ruins of a temple and some collected loose sculptures. Water represented by the sea and rivers was specially venerated here.

Geophysical Information:

The rocks at Punjeri & Mamallapuram are geologically very old and this region is not far from paleolithic sites which date back to 100,000 B.C.. Quarried sand being supplied to Chennai city contains pebbles some of which are fossilized rocks and others are core tools. These include choppers, borers and axes which have resemblance to the Acheulean and Oldowan Choppers.

Most of this sand is being quarried from river valleys near Tiruttani which is close to Pre-historic sites and situated about 80 Kms. west of Chennai. Modern studies have proved Milankovitch's theory that the climate has varied as a result of the earth's orbital deviations. Hence three overlapping cycles of 20,000, 40,000 & 1,00,000 years occur. This was proved by studies in 1970 of two cores from southern Indian ocean. By measuring the amount of heavy oxygen (oxygen-18 isotope) in a layer of sediment, a geological timetable of glacial and interglacial periods was arrived at. The sea level would be lower during maximum glaciation. Geologically Mamallapuram is submerging since the pre-historic times.

Contact with other Civilizations:

About 18,000 years ago the last major glaciation had reached its maximum. The sea-levels were lower and Sri Lanka was joined to India. In the Deccan the area between 12°-15°N Lat. was rain forest and the land south of 12°N and North of 15°N Lat. was grass, shrub and dry woodland and open woodland and forest extended further north. Saharan Africa on the Tropic of Cancer was wet grassland with climate similar to the Indus Valley which is also on the same latitude. About 10,000 years ago the climate changed during the Holocene period. This change was gradual with warm & cool periods. Glaciers retreated and the sea level rose gradually. Sahara began getting drier and the people living here migrated southward occupying the sub-Saharan region and the Nile delta in what is now Ethiopia. The Indus valley plain on the same latitude as sub-Saharan Africa has been silting since pre-historic times owing to river deposits and sudden floods caused by land slides impounding water in the Himalayas. This along with rising sea levels would have buried and submerged the earlier settlements along the coast. This region is an earthquake prone area.

It is probable they knew how to produce iron from rocks containing iron ore. As these people were sea-faring and traded with other civilizations including the East

Fig. 18 : SKETCH—COMPARISON

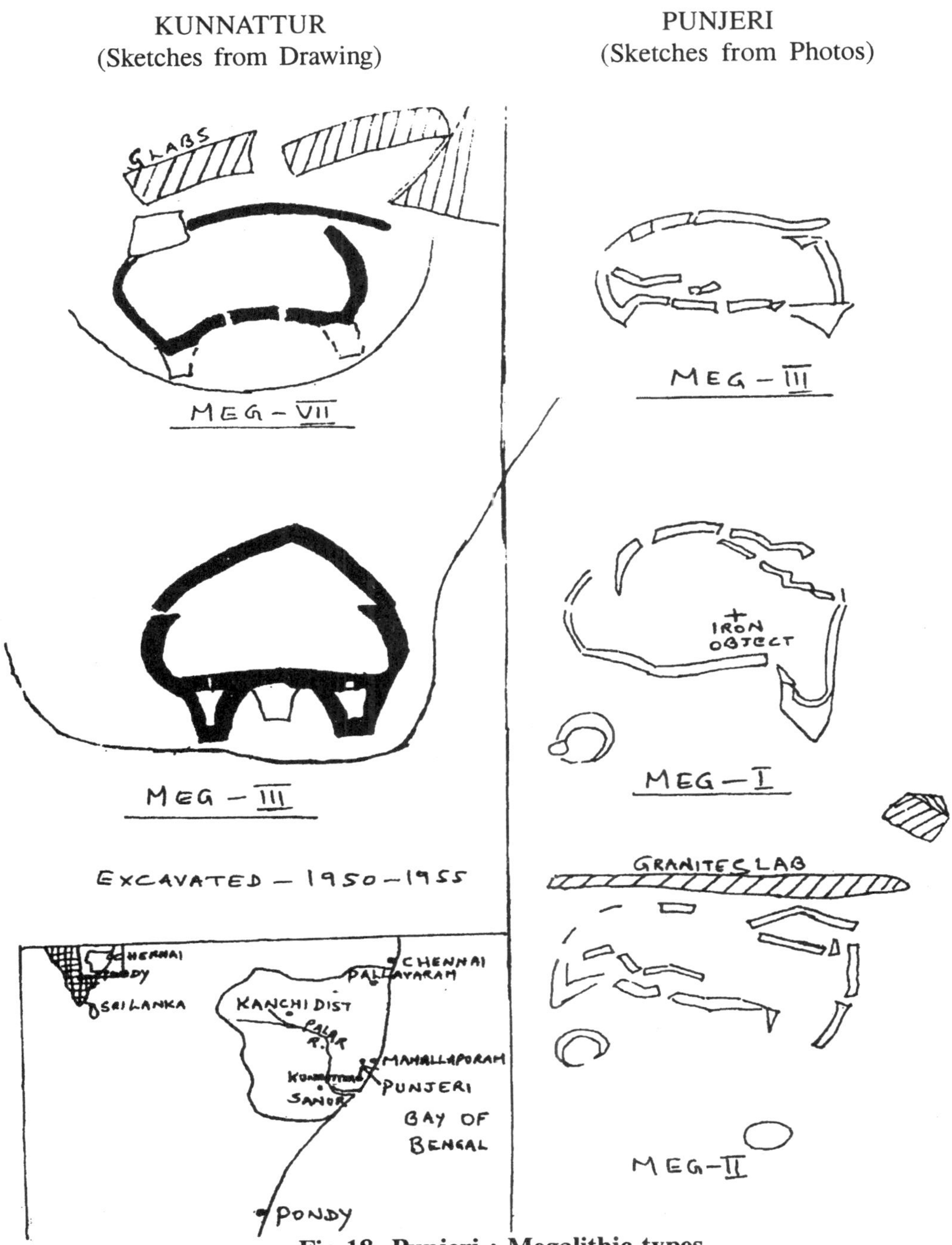

Fig 18. Punjeri : Megalithic types

coast, iron-working technology may have developed there or may have been learned from else where. Recent studies indicate that the early Harappans had close skeletal affinities with the Decccan chalcolithic people. By about 600 B.C. the sub-Saharan Africans were smelting iron and seem to have gone straight from using stone tools to iron ones. This they may have learnt from the Phoenicians who had trading posts in Eastern Mediterranean to trade with the Sumerians who also had earlier traded with the Indus Civilization since ancient times. It is probable that the change in climate, rising sea levels and massive floods would have scattered the Indus Civilization with migrations southward along the coasts. Many of these changes, though gradual, initially would have been cataclysmic too. Size diminution of domestic animals which has been noticed in the Indus Valley region is also seen on the East Coast.

In recent times microliths have been found on the hillock at Mahabalipuram. There are also remains of stones in roughly circular formation and unfinished excavation sites here. Indian Archaeology-A Review, published in 1957 mentions that protruding rocks near Krishna Mantappa (Eastern part of hillock) were removed for easy flow of rain water. The Pallava monuments at Mahabalipuram are dated to seventh century A.D. onwards. Prior to this the Eastern slopes of the hillock and the nearby areas could have had megaliths and structures especially Buddhist or Jaina, the traces of which may still be found while others may have been cleared. When the sea-level was lower, this area would have been a rocky promontory with arable land on the northern and southern sides and the eastern sides of the rocky outcrops suitable for megalithic burials. The change in climate would have led to change in way of life of primitive peoples here. As climate warmed and rain forest shrank, a change from nomadic to pastoral way of life could have taken place. Urbanization and sea trade would develop by contact with other civilization and result in sudden innovations in culture.

References

1. *Indian Archaeology*—1957, A Review.
2. *Maclean, Manual of the Administration of the Madras Presidency.*
3. Time life Books, *The Earth.*
4. Roger Coote, *Journey through Ancient Civilizations.*
5. *National Geographic Magazine*, October 1988.
6. M.S. Krishnan, *Geology of Indian & Burma.*
7. Purushotham Singh, *Burial Practices in Ancient India,* 1970.
8. *Survey of India Map.*
9. Possehl, *Indus Valley Civilization.*

10

Mughal Silver Coins From Bhikshi, Maharashtra

—*Dr. G.S. Khwaja**

Twelve (12) silver coins of Mughal King Muhammad Shāh (1719-48 A.D.) were discovered at village Bhikshi, in Chamorshi Tahsil of Gadchiroli District in Maharashtra State. These coins were found in 2005 while digging at the ancestral house of Shri Ghanshyam Pandurang Walke for its reconstruction. As a matter of legal formality the small treasure was confiscated by the district administration authority and in the course of their identification the same was sent by the Collector of Gadchiroli District to the Office of the Director (Epigraphy), Arabic and Persian Inscriptions, Archaeological Survey of India, Nagpur, where it is still kept for study.

The coins are in a good state of preservation, only one or two are little tarnished possibly because of their direct contact with the soil, for a period of time.

All the coins are silver pieces, round in shape with an average diametre of 22 cms. and weight of 11 grams.

So far as the issuing authority is concerned they have been issued by the Mughal King Muhammad Shah Badshah Ghazi who ruled India from Delhi throne since A.H. 1131/1718 A.D. to A.H. 1161/1748 A.D.

There is an interesting aspect of the history of numismatics of later-Mughal period in Central India, specially during the period of Maratha domination in erstwhile Berar, Central Indian State of Nagpur including other parts of the country, that when central Mughal King at Delhi became weak, authority to strike coins in the name of the king was given to regional and feudatory chiefs.

The *do-amali* (i.e. dual-governance) system in administrative set-up of Berar had already made Maratha Confederacy strong enough to demand rights to strike coins

* Epigraphy Branch, Archaeological Survey of India, Old High Court Building, Nagpur-440001

on behalf of the central Mughal Kings of Delhi, which was fulfilled with the conditin of recognizing authority of the king on the obverse side and have mint marks and other signs of the regional chief on the reverse. The Maratha Chiefs of Nagpur who were titled as Bhosla Rajas of Nagpur thus got the authority to strike coins at their different mints spread over their territory from Surat to Cuttack and Betul to Chandrapur.

The coins in reference is a good specimen of above mentioned conventional arrangement between the Mughal King Muhammad Shah and Bhosla Rajas of Nagpur.

If the date of these silver issues is taken into consideration we can safely say that they were minted by Bhosla King Raghuji I (1730-55 A.D.) of Nagpur after seeking permission from Mughal King Muhammad Shah.

These coins can be classified on the basis of their dates and mints. Of them two pieces are the issues of regnal year 12 of Muhammad Shah (corresponding to A.H. 1142-43 = 1729-30 A.D.) with the mint name Katak (i.e. Cuttack in Orissa). The rest 10 are of regnal year 27 of the king (corresponding to A.H. 1157-58 = 1744-45 A.D.) with the mint name Surat (in Gujarat). There is a slight difference between the legends on the both the sets.

The legends are in Persian in the customary style of the Mughal rulers. The obverse side, as per the tradition, contains name of the Mughal king and Hijri date whereas reverse side contains *san-e-julus* i.e. regnal year, mint-name and certain mint marks to signify the regional identity. The Hijri date which generally appears beneath the name of the king on obverse side in invariably out of flan in all the cases except Nos 1 & 2 where first two digits of hundred i.e. (11 xx) are readable.

The legends are as under :

Obverse

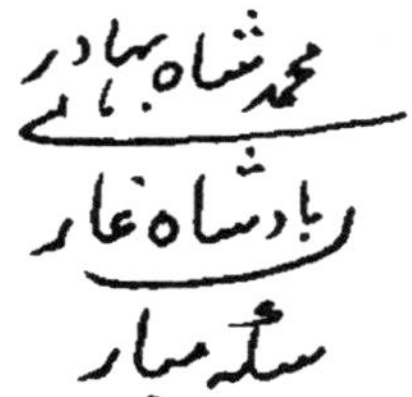

(Sikka-i-mubārak-i-Muhammad Shāh Bādshah Ghāzī Bahādur.)

Reverse

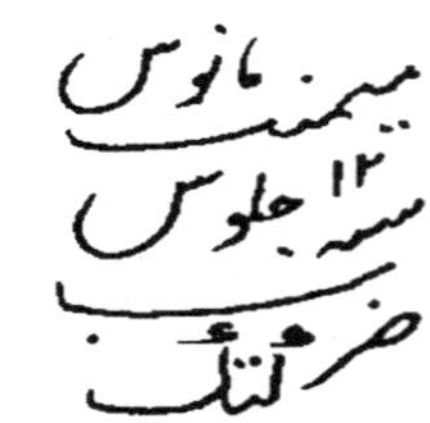

(San-i-julūs-i-maimanat mānūs. Darb-i-Katak)

One special feature with these issues which is to be noted that the names of the mints viz. Katak (Cuttack) and Surat with the A.H. dates and regnal years imprinted on them are not exactly the ones on which they were minted and issued. In fact these coins were struck, as per the available historical data, at Chanda (now Chandrapur in Maharashtra) mint by faithfully copying the coins of Muhammad Shah minted in his regnal 12 at Cuttack and at Surat in his regnal year 27. These pieces alongwith other coins were struck and issued time and again during the time of Bhosla Rajas of Nagpur.

The legends are as under :

Obverse

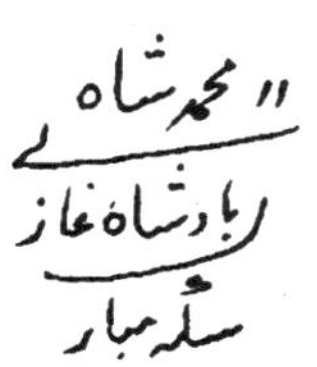

(Sikka-i-mubārak-i-Muhammad Shāh Bādshah Ghāzī II[XX])

Reverse

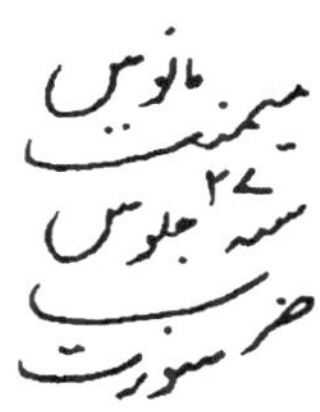

(San-i-julūs-i-maimanat mānūs. Darb-i-Surat Mint-mark : u)

11

A Unique Buddhist Image From Tewar – A Re-appraisal

*—Dr. Jalaj Kumar Tiwari**

The unique Buddhist sculpture under discussion was discovered at Tewar, a village about 12 km. to west of Jabalpur on the Jabalpur-Bheraghat road in Jabalpur district of Madhya Pradesh. This village has been identified as famous ancient city of Tripuri. (Pl.)

In early medieval period Kalachuri dynasty of Tripuri branch ruled over north-east Madhya Pradesh formerly known as Dahala between 8th to 13th century A.D. Their capital was Tiripuri.

During the reign of Kalachuri monarch Tiripuri rose to become an important centre of plastic art as evidenced by the good number of Saiva, Vaisnava, Sakta, Jain and Buddhist images found here. Kalachuri period in M.P. is well known to have been marked by the rise of art known as the Dahala school of art. The Kalachuri artists prepared numerous stone sculptures of Brahmanical, Jain and Buddhist faith in between 9th and 12th century A.D. Almost all images are easy to identify but a Buddhist image which was difficult to identify was in possession of Thakur Kirtibhanu Rai, Malguzar of Hirapur, 5 miles from Tewar[1].

The image was first noticed by Cunningham[2] who described it as "The most perfect specimen of Buddhist sculpture of Vajrapani, seated under a canopy with his hands infront of his breast, with the fingers arranged in the posture of teaching, on the right and left are figures with *chauries* and garlands and two kneeling figures, that to the left holding 2 *Vajras* (thunderbolts), and the other to the right with his hands joined in adoration. On the pedestal is inscribed the Buddhist creed of "*Ye dhamma*..."

---

* Assistant Archaeologist, A.S.I., Excavations Branch II, Patna.

in large letters, which is followed by a longer inscription begining with the name of Vajrapani.".

After Cunningham this image was described by R.D. Banerji in his famous work "The Haihayas of Tripuri and their monuments." He rightly contradicted the view of Cunningham and mentioned it as unknown *Bodhisattva*. On page 93-94 of his Book he writes. "At another place in the same village, in an open air shrine, is to be found a Buddhist image wrongly called *Vajrapani*, by older archaeologist. The figure cannot be that of the *Bodhisattva*. *Vajrapani* as he does not hold the thunderbolt (*Vajra*) in his hands. The image is that of an unknown *Bodhisattva* of the *Mahayana* school, seated in the *Vajraparyanka* posture, under a cinqfoil arch, with two hands in the attitude of turning the wheel of law (*Dharmacakramudra*). No *Dhyani Buddha* is to be seen on his head dress. Two *Dhyani Buddhas, Amoghasiddhi* in the *abhaymudra* on the right and *Vairochana* in the *Dharmachakramudra* on the left are seated, one at each end of the cinqfoil arch and a male attendent stands on each side of the main figure with a flywhisk in their hands. The *Bodhisattva* is seated on a fully blown lotus flower, under which is the wheel of law on a low pedestal, with a deer couchant on each side. There is an inscription on the pedestal in three lines containing the Buddhist creed and a votive record begning with the words *Sri-Vajrapani-Mahabauddah-Sadhunama*. After four more letters we find the words *Mahadanapati Jitadama, Jitadama* was the name of a merchant who was the donor of this image.[3]".

The same author referred as a crowned *Buddha* in his book "Eastern Indian School of medieval sculpture". Banerjee wrote "These crowned *Buddhas* are also to be found among second class stelae representing eight principal incidents of the life of *Buddha*. Such specimens are common all over Bengal and Bihar. The second class stelae with the crowned *Buddha* as the main figure proves this conclusively. Such images are by no means confined to Bengal and Bihar, because they have also been discovered at Tewar and Tigowa/Tegowa in the Central Provinces[4]".

The identification of this image as a crowned *Buddha* may not be acceptable because in the images of crowned *Buddha*, eight principal events of his life called *asta-maha-pratiharya* also carved on the stelae around the main figure of *Buddha*, which are absent in the said image of Tewar. Depiction of two *dhayani* Buddhas are also uncommon on the crowned *Buddha* images.

The same image is described as *Bodhisattva Avalokitesvar* by Rahman Ali in the following words. "The image of *Budhisattva Avalokitesvara* is fou nd at Tewar which bears an inscription on its *pitha*. It is shown under a cinque-foil arch in *Vajraparyanka* posture. His hands are in *dharmacakramudra*. But the images of *dhyani Buddhas* are not shown upon his head dress. Two figures of *Buddhas*, i.e. *Vairocane*, in *dharmachOakramudra* on the left and *Amoghasiddhi* in *abhayamudra* on the right, on both the ends of cinque-foil, are depicted. The figure a male *comaradhari*, in standing posture, is shown on either side of *Bodhisattva* is seated upon a *kamala*. Under the seat of *Bodhisattva*, a *cakra* is shown flanked by couchant deer. Behind the deer a seated male figure is visible but defaced. *Bodhisattva* wears *kirita-mukuta, kundalas, haras* (the bigger *hara* contains five bigger beads in the centre), *keyuras, valayas and nupuras*. The inscriptions engraved on the *pitha* informs us that the image was produced under the patronage of a nun named *Dhenuva* who belonged to the *Mahayana* school. The name of donor is also mentioned in the inscription, i.e., *Mahasamanta-dhipati Jitadamana*, who was a *sadhu* (merchant). Palaeographically, this image may be placed in circa 11 century A.D."[25]

This image cannot be identified as a *Bodhisattva Avalokitesvara* because the iconographical features of the image does not match to any form of *Avalokitesvara* mentioned in *Sadhanamala* or *Nispannayogvali*. *Avalokitesvara* originated from the *dhyani Buddha Amitabha*, but absence of *Amitabha* and presence of *dhyani Buddhas Vairochana* and *Amoghasiddhi* also suggests that this images may not be identified as *Bodhisattava Avalokitesvara*.

This image has been refered as *Bodhisattava* by R.K. Sharma[6] but this identification is not sufficient.

Though the image previously refers to it as *Vajrapani*, unknown *Bodhisattva*, crowned *Buddha*, *Bodhisattva Avalokitesvara* etc., careful study of the iconographic details shos-that it has more resemblance with Buddhist god *Manjuvara*, a form of *Bodhisattava Manjusri*. *Manjusri* is a popular *Bodhisattva*. *Mahayanists* belive that the worship of *Manjusri* can confer upon them wisdom, retentive memory, intelligence and eloquence and enables them to master many sacreds criptures[7]. *Manjuvara* is a form of *Manjusri* who originated from five *dhyani Buddhas*. He is usually mentioned in the *lalita* or *ardhaparyanka* attitude on the back of lion. His two hands display *dharmachakramudra*, which is the eternal symbol of instruction on the secrets of *dharma*. He is decked with all ornametns and holding the stalks of one or two lotuseson which appears the *prajnaparmita* manuscript.

Sculptures of *Manjuvara* without lion vehicle[8] was also in vogue and he may also be shown in *Vajraparyanka* posture[9].

The image under discussion also displaying the *dharamchakramudra* and sitting in *vijraparyanka* pose. Although he does not have an effigy of five *dhyani Buddhas* on his crest, only two *Vairochan* and *Amoghasiddhi* on either side of the bejwelled deity may be noticed. He is not holding *prajnaparamita* (the symbol of knowledge) placed on the lotus but is replaced by the depiction of *dharmachakra* and *mṛgadaon* (deer park) in the pedastal which is symbolizing the expansion of knowledge.

The necklace containing the five bigger beads in the centre worn by the central figure from Tewar is also the very striking. As we know the iconography of *Manjusri* has been influenced by the Hindu god *Kartikeya*. I may draw the attention that few images of *Manjusri* recovered from Nalanda[10] have been shown wearing a necklace containing five objects, i.e. bead, tiger claw pendant, *chakra* suspended from central amulet, tiget claw pendant and bead placed on regular interval. Almost same type of necklace may also be seen in the *Kartikeya* image[11]. In case of Tewar image the artist replaced the 2 beads, two tiger claw pendants and a central amulet by five bigger beads.

The inscription on the pedastal of image also creates confusion. As per inscription this is the image of *Vajrapani*. In this connection the observation of Cunningham is very important. He observed a small figure on the stele holding two *vajras* (thunderbolts). It may be possible that the inscription may be for the small figure and not for the main figure.

It may be mentioned that in early medieval period Buddhism declined in Madhya Pradesh and different forms of *Bodhisattvas* were not very popular. Regarding minor discrepencies, it may be assumed that the original text was not known in their entirety. Discrepencies between textual description and representation on the plastic art are also not uncommon.

Thus a minute observation and analysis of this image would clearly reveal that the image found at Tewar represents *Manjuvara* a form of *Manjusri* and not *Vajrapani*, crowned *Buddha* or *Avalokitesvara*.

References

1. Hira Lal, *Inscription in the Central Provinces and Berar*, 1932, Nagpur, p. 39.
2. A. Cunningham, *Archaeological Survey of India, Reports,* Vol. IX, 9. 59.
3. R.D. Banerji, The Haildhayas of Tripuri and their Monuments, *Memoirs of the Archaeological Survey of India*, No.23, Calcutta, 1932, pp. 93-94.
4. R.D. Banerji, *Eastern Indian School of Medieval Sculpture*, New Delhi, reprint, 1981, p. 86.
5. Rahman Ali, *Art and Architecture of the Kalachuris*, Delhi, 1980, p.p-172-73.
6. R.K. Sharma, *The Kalachuris and their Times*, Delhi, 1980, p.-216.
7. B. Bhattacharyya, *The Indian Buddhist Iconography*, Calcutta (reprint), 1987, p. 100.
8. Ibid, p. 118.
9. Ibid, Fig. 85.
10. F.M. Asher, *The Art of Eastern Indian 300-800,* Oxford University Press, Delhi, 1980, plates 164, 166, 191.
11. Ibid, Plate 203.

12

The Vedic Script

—Dr. P.N. Phadke

It is well known that the Ṛg veda having more than ten thousand Hymins was comitted to memory and used for Yadnas for several centuries before the art of writing in Brahmi was invented around 600 B.C. It is proposed to show here that even before Brahmi the Sanskrit languaeg had a script which was used to record all the scriptures authored during the third Millennium before the discovery of Brahmi.

1. Recent excavations by the Excavations Branch Nagpur of Archaeology Survey of India at Bhirana near Hissar in Haryana, located in the valley of ancient river Sarasvati has thrown considerable light on the ancient Indian history and pushed back its date beyond 7000 years from today. This was the period when primitive man in hunter-gatherer state, using stone tools and hand-made pottery, settled on the banks of river Sarasvati. Slowly, he took to farming, learnt the use of wheel for turning pottery and other objects and started a settled life in the valley of Sarasvati and other rivers. He prayed before various forces of nature for his comforts and well-being. The surplus crop supported a class who compiled these verses and committed them to memory. These compilations called the Ṛg veda describe Sarasvati and other rivers directly flowing to the sea (7.5). Now from the study of satellite imagery we know that this period belonged to 4000 B.C. and beyond, when river Saraswati flowed through the deserts of Rajasthan. Slowly its flow declined, it stopped flowing after Hissar, turned from west 3000 B.C. and flowed for soemtime through the channels now known as Hakra-Nala. This situation has been accurately described in the Mahābhārata as Vinashan tirth, Kamyakvana with a desert and Dwaitavana and Sarasvati flowing with a full force.

2. By this time, several villages with surplus products were organized into trading

communities who used seals for recording dispatch and rec2eipt of goods in the Indus-Sarasvati basin as well as the Middle East. Excavations show the presence of several kingdoms such as the Sumer, Babylon, Mittani, Hittaite and Egypt beyond the Indus. All of them used seals, for recording their trade activity, now discovered during excavations. Similar seals were found at Bhirana.

3. From 300 B.C. the Egyptians started building pyramids with the help of slaves captured from the Shephardine tribes from Arabasthan. Their walls showed pictures called Hyroglyphs narrating certain events. This was the beginning of writing.

4. The Sumerians also developed an urge for writing and recording their business. They used different combinations of stylus for this purpose, pressing them on wet clay tablets dried, fired and preserved as records. This nail headed script called Cuneiform introduced many innovations in the Egyptian script and reduced the number of symbols from 600 to 111. It became popular everywhere and remained in use for 2000 years. The Babyloneans spoke a different language but still used Cuneiform for office use. Iran in 550 B.C. spoke Avestan which was a corrupt form of Sanskrit and should have used a script if any from India. But they also preferred Cuneiform and Greek for writing their eipgraphs. This bilingual use gave a clue to solve the riddle of Cuneiform script which was read back upto the Sumerian times of 3000 B.C. Excavations have delivered thousands of tublets belonging to this long period and their study has helped to reconstruct the history of the Middle East.

5. From 300 B.C., we find a spurt in the Vedic literature in the form of Yajur Veda, Samaveda, the Brahmana commentaries, Upanishad philosophy and many other books.

   It is impossible to memorize such a vast literature in prosaic form without the help of a writing method. Therefore, the problem arises whether (1) The Sanskrit had its own script and if so, why it was not used in the Middle East especially in Iran in 550 B.C. (2) If there was no such script why Cuneiform was not used on the Indian soil either on the Indus seals of clay tablets or epigrahs. Sumerians spoke a corrupt form of Sanskrit.

6. Around 1500 B.C., the Egyptians were defeated by the Hittaits from Turkey which had a disastrous effect on their polity. Construction of pyramid was stopped and slaves released from captivity. They returned to their motherland under the able guidance of Moses and settled in Israel. They wanted to record their sufferings in their Hebrew language for which a script was nec-

essary. They invented a new way of writing instead of using Cuneiform. They picked up certain symbols from the Indus seals which had a meaningful expression in Sumerian as well as in Sanskrit and formed Hebrew alphabets. Its first letter Alef showing two horns of a bull as V meant Sanskrit Balivarda-Bali-Ali-Aleph. Second letter Beth shown as a square meant Sanskrit Vastu-Bastu-Beth and meant a residence. Dr. S.R. Rao has shown 22 such symbols picked up from the Indus seals and used as letters in the Hebrew script which was subsequently used for writing Arabic. If so, why the same process could not be followed in respect of Sanskrit is the real problem.

7. A close review tells us that the Sanskrit grammarians had a deeper study of their language. They introduced separation of vowels and consonants. The latters were grouped into five sets, according to the place of their origin such as Velaras (Ka), Paletals (Cha), Retroflex (Ta), Dentals (Fa), Labials (Pa), Semi-vowels and Fricatives. Each set had four members with a phonetic symbold selected from the Indus seals and placed as first letter or Surd which changed to the next position by addition of a marker such as – or O. Thus, K, Ko, K-, K-o formed four letters K, Kh, Ga, Gha. Sixteen such symbols were selected from the Indus seals to form the Sanskrit script. They were Ka, Cha/Chha/Ja, Ta, ta/da, Na, Pa/Ba, Ma, Ra, La, Va, Sa/Sha. These symbols were merged in 32 Brahmi letters formed around 600 B.C. and identified by Cunningham and others from epigraphs. B.B. Lal has shown their presence on the Megalithic pottery.

8. The Brahmi script became a model classification for all Indian languages upto Sri Lanka in South, Tibet in North, and Myanmar and Laos in the far East-excepting Tamil which stuck to the original arrangement with 16 symbols. The Tamil grammar Tolkappiam states how the script was used as Granthic for writing purpose while they lived in the North before 600 B.C. and sage Agastya brought them to the South. The use of markers was dropped during the process of migration and Tamil script became a total confusion. It is not possible to read it without knowing the context. All the four phonems in a set such as Ka, Kha, Ga, Gha are represented by one *Surd* Ka, and are not intelligible.

9. How old might be this Vedic Sanskrit script? The Sumerians started writing in 3000 B.C. and the Indus people could have copied them in absence of their own script. So the Sanskrit script must have existed around 3000 B.C. when sage Vyasa composed first 8000 verses of the Mahabharata and other books. It must have prevailed upto the introduction of Brahmi in 600 B.C. when all texts must have been rewritten with the help of new script. Only Tamil contin-

ued its original form without markers and has lived with the confusion for the last 2500 years.

10. The omission of markers brought about a sea change in the form of spoken Sanskrit which gave birth to its corrupt forms such as Chulika Paisachi Prakrit in the North-West. One of its rule proposed dropping of third and fourth consonants.Thus, Ga, Gha, Ja, Jha were replaced by Ka, Kha, Cha, Chha. When these people migrated to Malwa a conditional further change proposed dropping of first letters K, Ga, Cha, Ja, Ta, da, Pa, Ya, Va which gave birth to Pali language. Similar changes resulted in formation of Tamil. The process was stopped with the introduction of Brahmi for all languages.

11. In conclusion, it may be stated that the Sanskrit had a script of its own since 3000 B.C. which needs deeper study.

References:

1. Vanished Civilization, *Readers, Digest*, 2002.
2. N. Mahalingam, *Ancient World*, Madras 1983, p. 261-277.
3. Mirashi V.V., *The Satvahanas*, Nagpur, 1981, p. 202, 282.
4. P.N. Phadke, *India through the Ages*, Nagpur, 2003.

13

New Archaeological Findings—An Overview[1]

—Jagat Pati Joshi[2]

I am most grateful to the organizers of this National Seminar on Archaeology and the Govt. of Chhattisgarh in particular for inviting me. It is a matter of great satisfaction, nay a matter of pride that the Chhattisgarh Govt. under its dynamic Chief Minister and Minister for Culture have kept archaeology and heritage in high priority because of which the Deptt. of Culture and Archaeology in the state is taking big strides. We archaeologist in a national level extend our heartiest felicitations and good wishes to this nascent deptt. and greatly admire its achievements in a short period. I congratulate Dr. A.K. Sharma, the Archaeological Advisor and his team for the excellent work done at Sirpur. May the team dig, discover, preserve and create right consciousness for the heritage. A pride in past always moulds the bright future.

This is also the time to remember with deep gratitude the great archaeologist late Dr. Moreshwar G. Dixit who first excavated and brought to light the Svastika Vihar and other Buddhist establishments at Sirpur, which is the most pioneering work done by this great savant of archaeology and opened a vista of archaeological discoveries in the present Chhatisgarh state.

It is a happy sign that for the better preservation of monuments of Chhatisgarh state the Archaeological Survey of India has opened a new circle at Raipur and we hope now the monuments of Chhatisgarh will have a better look and attention. We hope that in the next financial year Archaeological Survey of India would be able to bring out the book entitled *'Inventory of monuments of National Importance of Chhatisgarh'*. It is being made press ready.

Since this is a national seminar, I thought it appropriate, I should share with this angust gathering some of my thoughts on Harappan archaeology a subject which I

1. Inaugural address at the National Seminar at Raipur and Sirpur, Chhatisgarh on 25th and 26th March, 2007
2. Former Director General, Archaeological Survey of India.

have been persuing for the last 35 years besides other archaeological persuits. I would like to talk on some of the emerging trends of the Harappan archaeology.

The Harappan Civilization which flourished during the 3rd-2nd millennia BCE ranks amongst the four widely known civilizations of the Old World and covers appreciably larger area than in the early Dynastic Egypt or Sumer. Like the other Old World Civilizations, the Harappan civilization seems to have grown from the skilful utilisation of the fertile river systems and their valleys in the north-western region of the Indo-Pakistan subcontinent. The Harappans have given systematic town planning, fortification of citadels, elaborate drainage system, the idea of establishing of granaries and surplus economy, standardization of brick sizes, weights and measures, geometric instruments e.g. right angles, linear scale and plumb bob are the principal gifts of the Harappans to the succeeding cultures through the ages. It was the Harappan who gave the idea of welfare of the workers for the first time by establishing workmen's quarters and now it has become a necessity. Different types of hydraulic architecture is another legacy of the Harappans besides many other in social, economic and religious fields. Harappans opened new horizons in the west by establishing of long distant trade by sea and land.

There are now about 20 sites in the Indo-Pakistan subcontinent which provide a back-drop to the genesis of this great civilization in different ecological zones. It has developed in the triangle Rehman Dheri and Kotdij i in Pakistan to Kalibangan and Kunal in India.

The area of distribution of Harappan settlements runs broadly from Sutkagendor in Makran (Pakistan) and Desalpur and Dholavira in the west, Manda in southern Jammu (J&K) to Daimabad in southern Maharashtra and Hulas in Saharanpur district in U.P. (India). If sites in Pakistan are also included it covers an area of about two million sq. Kms. The excavated sites of Harapppa culture have yielded a substantial number of 14^{C} dates. As a result, the age range for the Harappa civilization is between *circa* 2600 to 2000 B.C.E.

For establishing distant trade, the Harappans had agricultural production, mineral wealth and consumer areas of Gulf of Oman, Persian Gulf and West Asia where Indian goods were in great demand. Let us quickly examine the Harappan economy agriculture, transport and industry which was the basis for internal and external trade.

In the third millennium BCE the western part of the IndoPakistan sub-continent had fertile land, watered by the Indus and Sarasvati with sufficient rainfall. The archeaobotanical studies carried on the samples of grains found during the excavations of the Harappan levels of the eastern zone show a variety of crops and throw considerable light on the food habits of the people. The large extra produce was kept in public granaries and also in the houses in large jars. Wheat and barley were the principal cereals eaten by the people *millet, ragi, kodon, jawar* were also eaten. Seasame and mustard were used as cooking medium and lighting the lamps. Cotton was widely grown and was exported also. Agriculture was practiced in the fertile riverine valleys having vast tracts of rich alluvium brought by the snowfed rivers emanating from the Himalayas. Tilling was done with a wooden plough having a copper capping at the head of the ploughshare. It could be of a type which is available in terracotta models found at Mohenjodaro, Banawali and Kalibangan. The evidence of ploughed field found in the Early Harappan levels at Kalibangan gives a good picture of two sets of furrows crossing each other at right angles in a grid pattern. It appears the Harappans also practiced a system of having double crops in a field as is done in Rajasthan now-a-days where mustard is grown in wide distanced furrows and have horsegram grown in the narrower ones.

Mostly, the Harappans depended for their agriculture on the alluvial soil and the canal water. Monsoon has been an uncertain factor in the Indo-Pakistan sub-continent since time immemorial and because of this factor, perhaps the Harappan were forced to dig canals to be assured of permanent supply of water which could be utilized for large area of agricultural activity and could be used for single or double cropping pattern. Francfort, Gentelle and ASI discovered a canal in the Haryana region and stratigraphically it belonged to the Harappan period. At Baror in Rajasthan a U shaped canal has been found recently. The digging of moat around the Harappan settlement at Banawali and the canal connecting the river Bhogavo with the dock-yard at lothal are other examples. The evidence from Allahdino suggests that the Harappans knew well irrigation. According to Fairservis, Harappans were 'master hydraulic engineers' .

The economic boom brought by agriculture and its surplus food produce kept in granaries, long distance internal and external trade and exploitation of natural and marine produce brought prosperity leading to planned monumental architecture in brick and stone, development of various crafts, establishment of merchant guilds in various regions of the' Cultural empire of Harappans in the Indo-Pakistan Sub-continent.

The Harappans were great hydraulic engineers. They were known for their wells and canal irrigation. Wells are found at various sites. Construction of check dams at Dholavira, storm water and city drainage system in Harappan towns and cities are found. The Dockyard at Lothal, Great Bath Complex at Mohenjodaro are fine examples of water bodies.

Earlier no temple was found at Mohenjodaro and Harappa. Now the scenario is changing. At Edith Shahr Complex, a Zaggurat type of structure having atop a platform with drains, at Damb Saddat evidence of a stone platform with drains and stone cairn with a skull, at Kalibangan fire altars and a sacrificial cistern with animal bones and bathing platforms, fire altars at Lothal and an apsidal fire temple like structure at Banawali lead to emergence of religious architecture of Harappans.

For trade and movement of people, transport is very important. Animal remains of camel, elephant, horse and ass from Harappan sites testify their use for transport of men and material. The evidence of exotosis and ancylosis in cattle bones at Surkotada suggests that they were used for draft purposes. Bullock carts and animal packs were used. A variety of cart frames and wheels with or without hubs suggests that the bullock cart was the most popular mode of transport of Harappans. They also used spoked wheels. The find of small models of boats from Lothal and depiction of boat in a seal from Mohenjodaro and on a potsherd from Dhulia suggests boats with or without sails and a cabin for the crew. Multioared boat on a potsherd from Lothal is another type. S.R. Rao discovered five terracotta models of boats from Lothal. Flat bottomed boats were used for transport in rivers and lakes.

Crow was a popular bird amongst the Harappans. This bird was used as marine direction finder. In high seas crows were flown from the deck of the ship or boat to find the nearby land. In case the land is there the crow will not return to the ship. In case of no land it would return to the ship/boat. The Harappan seals clearly show two crows on its deck.

Besides, crow was a very clever bird. In one of rare depiction of a story of thirsty crow and again a crow and jackal from Lothal, the artist besides depicting the intelligence of crow in art has told story to children. Later we know during the historical times Vishnu Sharma had given the same story in *Panch Tantra* also but this depiction of fable is of very early date in Harappan contest.

The architecture of the port town at Kuntasi, Gujarat had a double fortification with a watch tower/or light house for guiding the vessels. This could be an important guiding point to sailors. Since the Harappans planned their streets on cardinal directions, they could perhaps knew the Polar Star which was of considerable help in navigation also.

Shell compass of 45° and 30° are found in the excavations at Lothal, Dholavira and Bagesara. Since the streets follow the cardinal directions, knowledge of north from the Polar Star could perhaps guide the night navigation. Geometrical instruments like scales, plumb-bob, right angles of the Harappans used for town planning. They followed decimal system. Weight and measures. Evidence of hour glass at Kalibangan is remarkable. House building of structures as practiced by Harappans was discovered, besides mortar, bonding, plaster, decorated tiled pavement of the rooms of the houses, doors and windows and various types of kilns used by Harappans have been found.

The recent excavations of Lahuradeva, U.P. has opened an new horizon of Neolithic cultures of Ganga Valley. The excavations of Bhirrana, Haryana has pushed back the date of Harappa Culture to 4th-5th millennium B.C.

The excavations of Loteshwar and Padri has given a preHarappan horizon to the area of Saurashtra. The excavation at Sunauli has given unique necropolis of late Harappan culture with double and triple burials and the custom of burying of swords in burials.

In the field of historical archaeology, the excavations at Mansar has given remains of both religious and secular architecture from 2nd century. B.C. to 7th century A.D. and plethora of material of the Vakataka period along with a palace and a large number of superb sculptures of Vakataka art have been found. Similarly the remains uncovered at Sirpur has revealed religious tolerance and freedom of worship of different religious cults Brahmins, Saivas, Buddhists in the 7-8th centuries. Sirpur was a very big archaeological complex. What ever has come out is just a beginning of many more discoveries.

It is necessary that some of the state department of Archaeology in India may need reorganization to cope with the inclusion of new monuments and museums and archaeological gardens. For this there is a necessity of training of persons in excavations, epigraphy, conservation and museology. The Institute of Archaeology of ASI may play pivotal role of short term intensive training courses. In archaeology, field training in excavation and conservation is a must. It should be our utmost endeavor to have highly trained and skilled people to look after our rich heritage. It is a technical work which should be looked after by professionals only.

Awareness for the preservation of heritage is to be inculcated in the schools and heritage walks may be taken by NGOs so that people are taken round of monument and appreciate its architectural beauty and history. It is the people who are the best custodians of our heritage and their involvement and active participation is the best guarantee for the preservation of monuments. Village Panchayats and local associations can look after and maintain the unprotected monuments in the neighbourhood. NGOs could give motivation in this respect.

I have great pleasure to inaugurate this Seminar and look forward for a very fruitful discussion on new discoveries in India and discoveries in Chhattisgarh. *Vāde Vāde Jāyete Tattvabodah.*

Thank you.

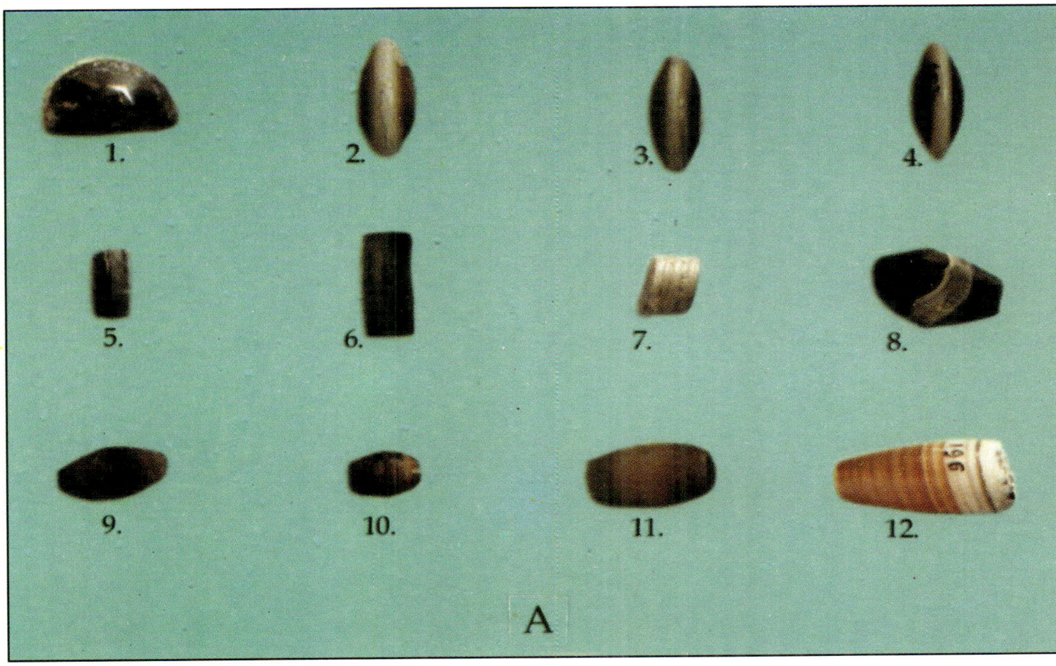

Plate IA. Mahisdal Beads.

Plate IB. Mahisdal Beads.

Plate IIA. Sirpur-Mahasivagupta Balarjuna's residence.

Plate IIB. Sirpur-Mahasivagupta Balarjuna's seal.

Plate IIIA. Sirpur-Bird's eye view of *Baleshwar* temple complex.

Plate IIIB. Sirpur-Yugal Siva Temple.

Plate IVA. Sirpur-Siva Temple (SRP-9).

Plate IVB. Sirpur-Siva Temple facing west (SRP-7).

Plate VA. Sirpur-SivaTemple with Star Shaped *Garbha-griha* (SRP-8).

Plate VB. Sirpur-Siva Linga with *Nava-graha* pedestal.

Plate VIA. Sirpur-Ganga and Yamuna in (SRP-7).

Plate VIB. Sirpur-Kartikeya in (SRP-8)

PlateVIIA. Sirpur-Lion figure in (SRP-8).

Plate VIIB. Sirpur-Inscription from *Baleshwar* Temple.

Plate VIIIA. Punjeri-Sarcophagus

Plate VIIIB. Punjeri-Dolmen

Obverse

Reverse

1-2 : Silver coins from Katak mint.

Obverse

Reverse

3-4 : Silver coins from Surat mint.

Plate IX. Kwaja, Mughal coins

Plate X. Tewar-Buddhist Sculpture, Stone 11 Century A.D.